I0419055

SANDRINE PELISSIER

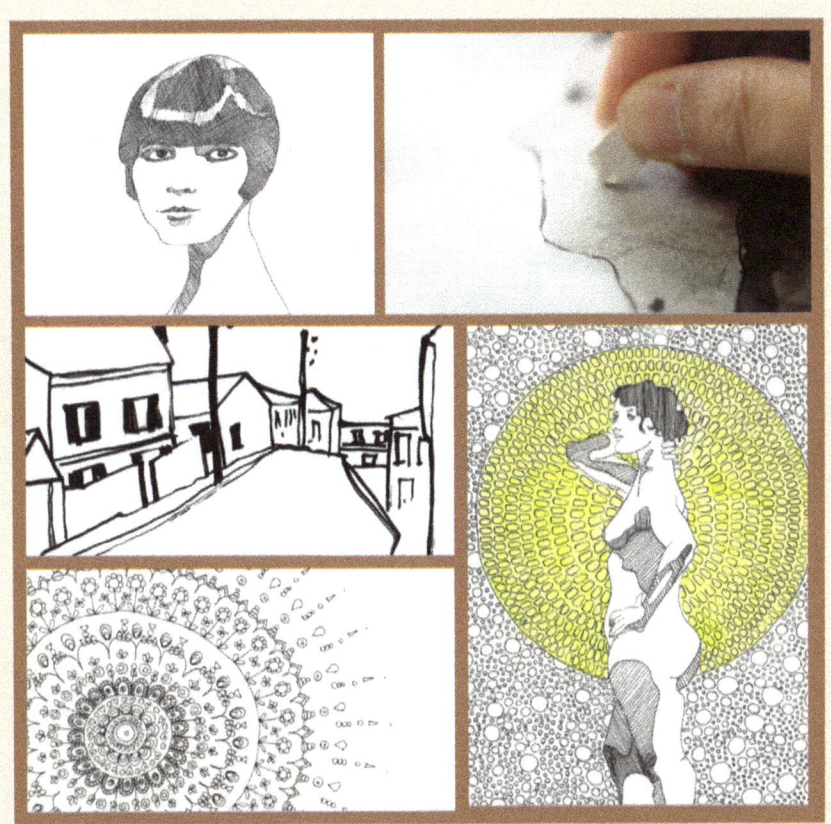

A CREATIVE EXPLORATION
of DRAWING

YOUR DRAWING STYLE IS AS UNIQUE AS YOUR HANDWRITING—LET'S FIND IT!

Get inspired to draw with step-by-step tutorials and endless ideas.
Drawing shouldn't be intimidating—it should be fun!

Published by:
Library Tales Publishing
www.LibraryTalesPublishing.com
www.Facebook.com/LibraryTalesPublishing

Copyright © 2025 by Sandrine Pelissier
Published by Library Tales Publishing, New York, NY

No part of this publication may be reproduced, stored in a retrieval system, or transmitted in any form or by any means, electronic, mechanical, photocopying, recording, scanning, or otherwise, except as permitted under Sections 107 or 108 of the 1976 United States Copyright Act, without the prior written permission of the Publisher.

Requests to the Publisher for permission should be addressed to the Legal Department, 1-800-754-5016; Legal@LibraryTales.com.

Trademarks: Library Tales Publishing, Library Tales, the Library Tales Publishing logo, and related trade dress are trademarks or registered trademarks of Library Tales Publishing, Inc. and/or its affiliates in the United States and other countries, and may not be used without written permission. All other trademarks are the property of their respective owners.

For general information on our other products and services, please contact our Customer Care Department at 1-800-754-5016, or fax 917-463-0892. For technical support, please visit www.LibraryTalesPublishing.com

Library Tales Publishing also publishes its books in a variety of electronic formats. Every content that appears in print is available in electronic books.

** PRINTED IN THE UNITED STATES OF AMERICA **

9798894410241

INTRODUCTION

I believe drawing should be fun—without too many rules. The key to improving is simple: draw as much as you can. This book will be your guide to rediscovering the joy of drawing and exploring different creative paths.

Beyond classical and realistic styles, there are countless ways to draw. This book will help you express yourself freely and enjoy the wonderful world of drawing.

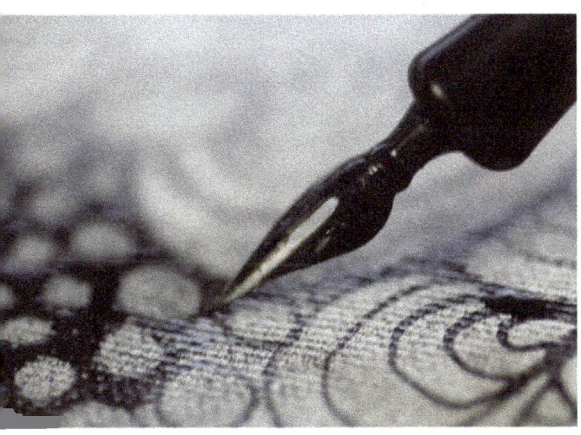

Drawing books can sometimes feel intimidating—especially if the skill level seems out of reach for beginners or occasional artists. But this book is different. With accessible, step-by-step techniques, it offers a satisfying experience for artists of all levels.

This is the book for you if:

- You want to explore different drawing styles.
- You prefer learning by doing rather than reading.
- You enjoy hands-on assignments.
- You want to be inspired to create your own ideas.
- You're excited about drawing.
- You don't want overly technical, hyper-realistic instructions.
- You believe drawings don't have to be classical to be interesting.

ABOUT THE AUTHOR

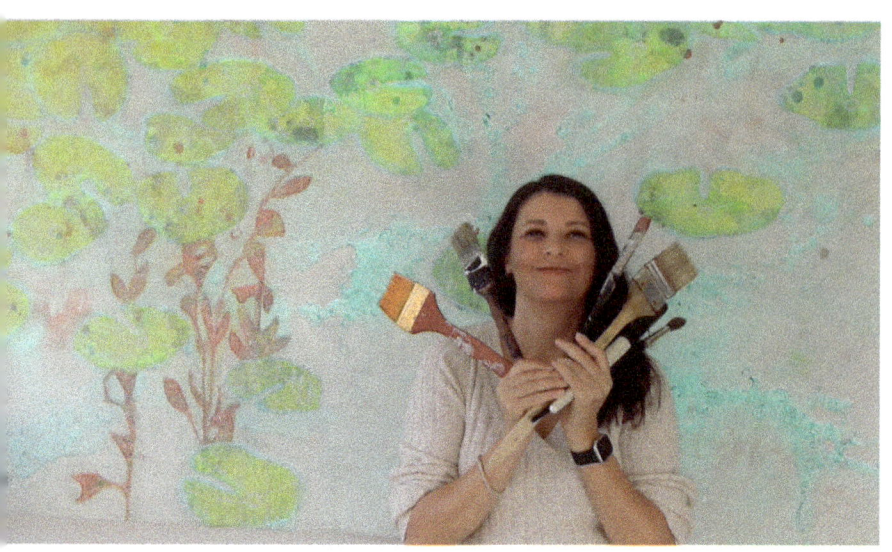

Originally from France, Sandrine Pelissier has lived in North Vancouver, Canada, for the past 23 years.

Her work has been extensively exhibited and collected throughout Canada and internationally. She is also part of the Vancouver Art Gallery's Art Rentals and Sales program.

Many of her paintings have been featured in art books and magazines, including *Artist Magazine, Watercolor Artist Magazine, Acrylic Magazine,* and *International Artist Magazine.* In addition to her artwork, she has authored two art instruction books: *Fearless Watercolor for Beginners: Adventurous Painting Techniques to Get You Started* and *Painting Imaginary Flowers: Beautiful Blooms and Abstract Patterns in Mixed Media.*

For the past seven years, Sandrine has been writing for her blog, PaintingDemos.com, which reaches about 20,000 monthly visitors and has a mailing list of approximately 10,000 subscribers.

An active member of her community, she co-founded the North Shore Art Crawl and a weekly life drawing group. She also served as a board member of the North Vancouver Arts Council for seven years and has been invited as a juror for public art projects, art grants, and juried exhibitions.

CONTENTS

Introduction 3

About the Author 4

Chapter 1:   Drawing With Your Non-dominant Hand & Blind Contour Drawing . . .7
  Continuous Blind Contour Drawing 8
  2- Continuous Drawing With Your Non-dominant Hand 9

Chapter 2:   Wreck Your Drawing With an Eraser 13
  Start by making a drawing from life, imagination, or a reference picture . . 14
  Once you are happy with your drawing, start erasing it 15

Chapter 3:   Simple Geometric Patterns & Zentangles 17
  Simple Mandalas 20
  Adding Patterns to Sketches, Life Drawings, & Portraits 22
  Yupo Postcard with Watercolor & Marker Doodles 24

Chapter 4:   Going Digital 27
  Online Sketching Tools 28
  Sketching On an iPad 28

Chapter 5:   It's All About the Shade 31

Chapter 6:   Selective Coloring 35

Chapter 7:   Making Waterproof Paper 41
  A Yupo Paper Alternative 42
  Painting a Still Life with
  Gel-Covered Paper 45

Chapter 8:   Comparing Different Media & Styles 49
  The Original Drawing 50
  Using Charcoal & White Acrylic Paint 50
  Using Watercolor Pencils 51
  Using Watercolor Washes & A Black Outline 51
  5- Using Black Markers & Watercolor Crayons
  (Inspired by Henri de Toulouse Lautrec) 51
  Using Marker & Watercolors (Inspired by Egon Schiele) 52
  Markers & Watercolors on Yupo Paper 52

Chapter 9: Stamping Text onto Paintings or Drawings 53

Stamping with Letters 54

Stamping with a Pencil Eraser 55

Chapter 10: The Beautiful Contrast of Lines and Washes 57

Chapter 11: Figure Drawing 63

Using Several Pencils At Once 64

Drawing Without Lifting Your Pencil 65

Drawing With a Stick 65

Beauty is Confidence, Not Perfection 66

Variety Is the Spice of Life (Drawing) 67

Chapter 12: Between Drawing and Painting 71

Adding Patterns to Your Painting 72

Drawing Lines On Canvas 73

Drawing with Pencil, Charcoal, or Dry Brush on Canvas 74

Using a Drawing Medium as Paint 77

Chapter 13: Simple Monoprint Techniques 79

The No-Phone Selfie 80

Monoprints on Plexiglass 82

Chapter 14: Drawing From an Abstract Background 85

Painting an Abstract Background 86

Identifying and Outlining Shapes 87

Negative Painting with Acrylic 87

Refining and Adding Details 87

Chapter 15: Creative Shading 89

Cross-hatching 90

Hatching with Parallel Lines 91

Contour Lines 91

Scribbling 92

Stippling 93

Zentangles and Patterns 93

Chapter 16: Doodling Over Magazine Pages 95

CHAPTER 1

Drawing With Your Non-dominant Hand & Blind Contour Drawing

Let's get started with something a bit different from what we usually think of when we think about drawing. Sometimes, all we need to be creative is to let go of expectations. We'll begin with a **continuous blind contour** drawing. I will ask you to draw or paint something without looking at your paper or lifting your marker or pencil. Then, you'll try drawing with your non-dominant hand. If you want to get adventurous, you can even try drawing with your mouth or foot!

look at the object you want to draw, place your drawing tool on the paper, and draw the object *without* looking at your paper or lifting your utensil. KKeeping your drawing tool in constant contact with the paper will make it easier to draw without looking. The result will be a drawing made from one continuous line.

In this exercise, you'll use your dominant hand—but because you won't be looking at your drawing, the results may look strange. That's okay! This exercise is meant to train you to truly observe what you're drawing instead of focusing too much on the paper.

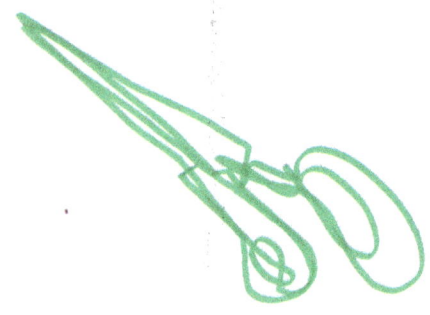

You Will Need
- Printer or drawing paper
- Markers, washable felts, or pencils
- Something to draw (an object in your house, a person, or a photo)

Continuous Blind Contour Drawing

We'll begin with a continuous blind contour drawing. Here, the rule is simple:

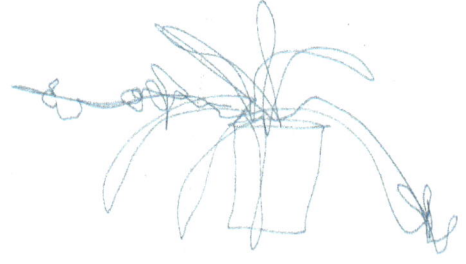

Blind contour drawings: a pair of scissors and a plant

2- Continuous Drawing With Your Non-dominant Hand

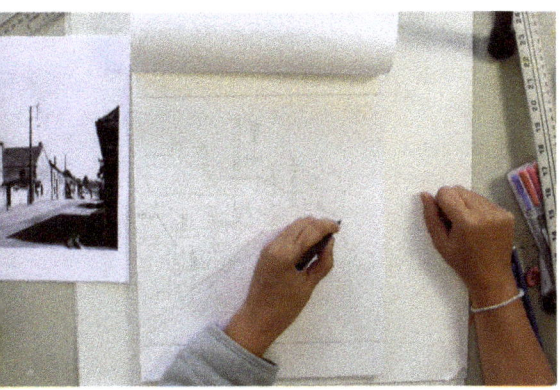

I encourage you to try this technique using reference pictures, still life, or people as your subjects.

Now, let's create a continuous line drawing with your non-dominant hand. This exercise is similar to the previous one, but this time, since you are using your non-dominant hand, you can look at the paper while you draw.

The key here is to keep your drawing tool in constant contact with the paper, just as you did in the blind contour drawing. The result will be a single, continuous line that forms your drawing.

Here are a few examples of continuous non-dominant-hand drawings:

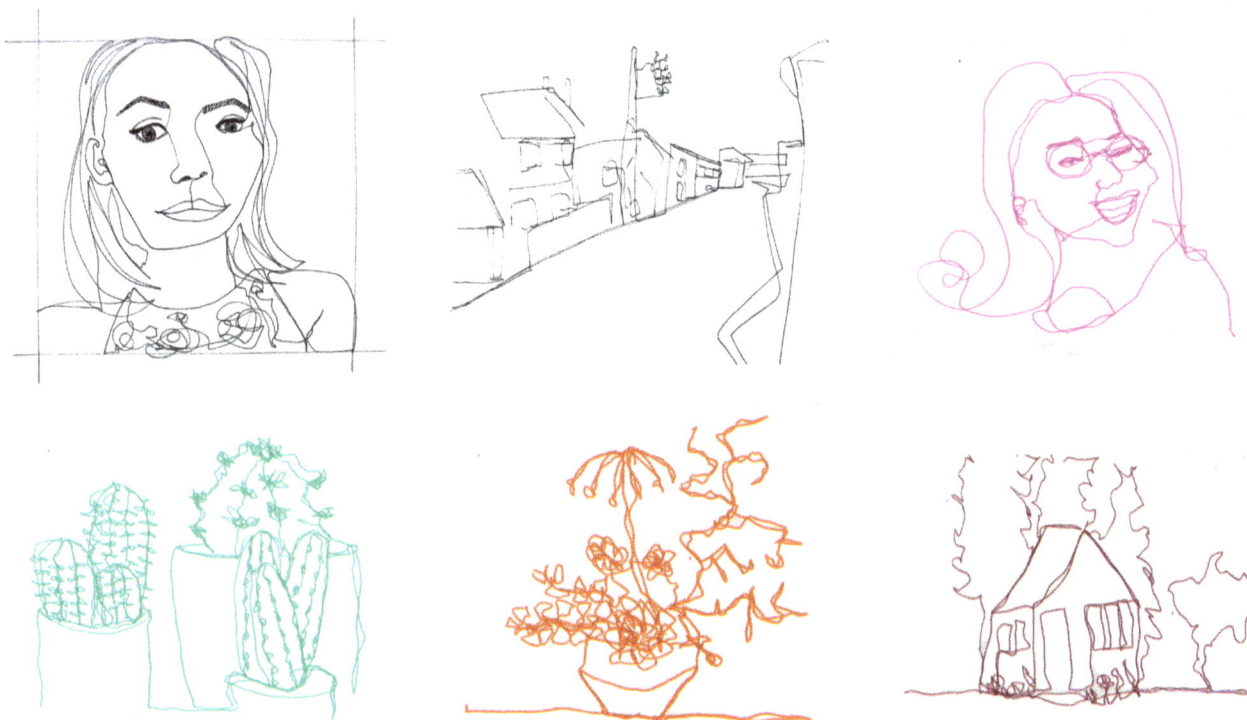

 TIP:
Try Incorporating non-dominant-hand drawing into a regular (dominant-hand) drawing.

Examples of how you can incorporate elements of non-dominant-hand drawing into a regular drawing:

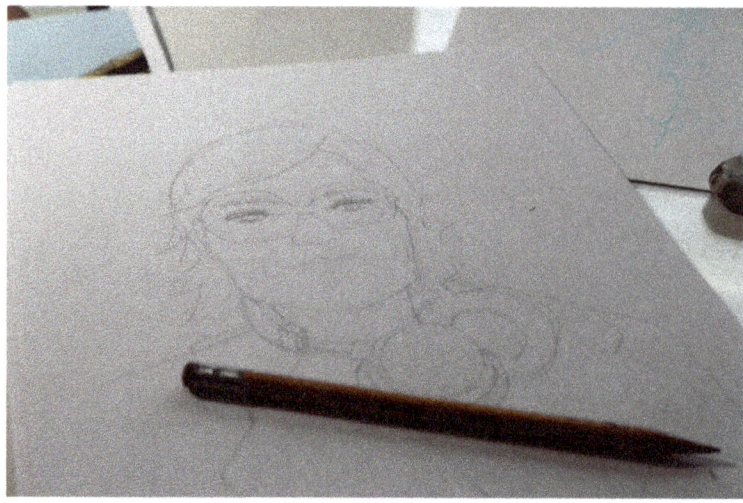

For this piece, I started with a simple line drawing of my daughter, which I created from a reference picture. I first sketched in pencil, allowing me to make corrections and erase if necessary. Once I was satisfied with the drawing, I went over the lines with a marker to finalize it.

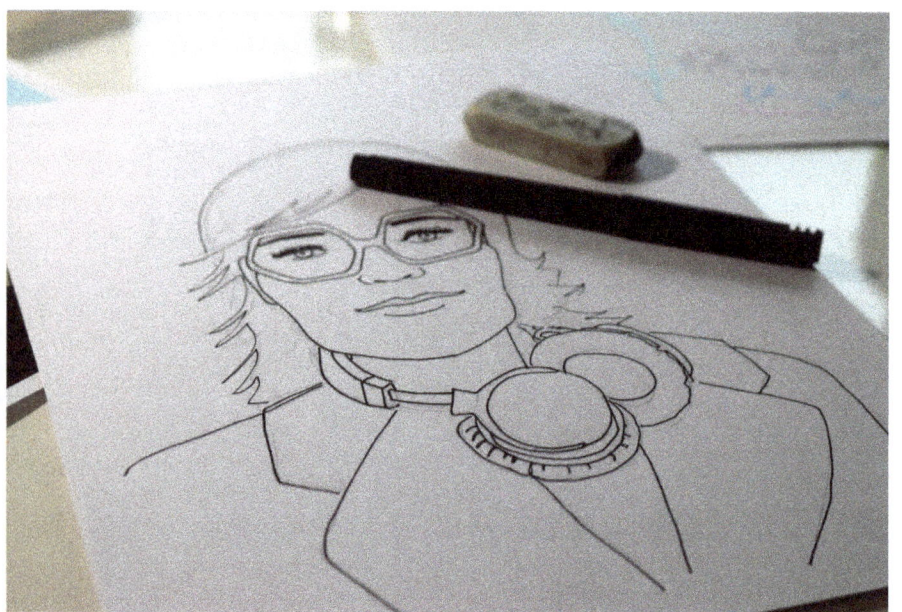

 TIP:
Once you have made a line drawing that you are satisfied with, scan it and print out copies to experiment with different ideas on the same drawing.

This is my original line drawing.

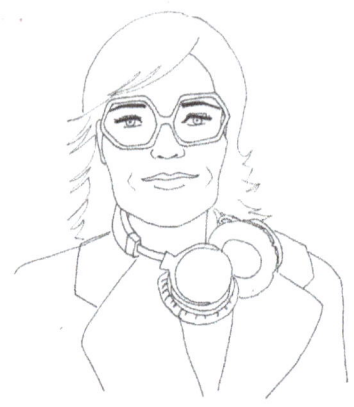

I scanned it and made copies with my printer so I could try different ways of adding elements with my non-dominant hand:

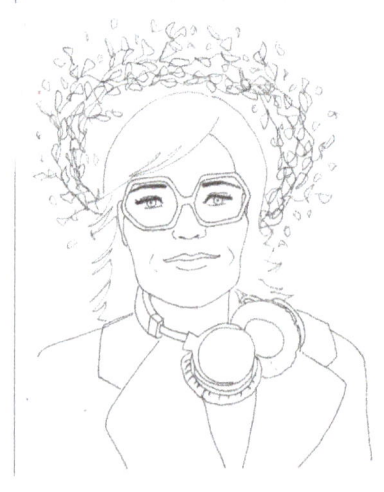

You can also try adding selective coloring to your drawing. Here, I used colored pencils. (Read more about selective coloring in Chapter 6.)

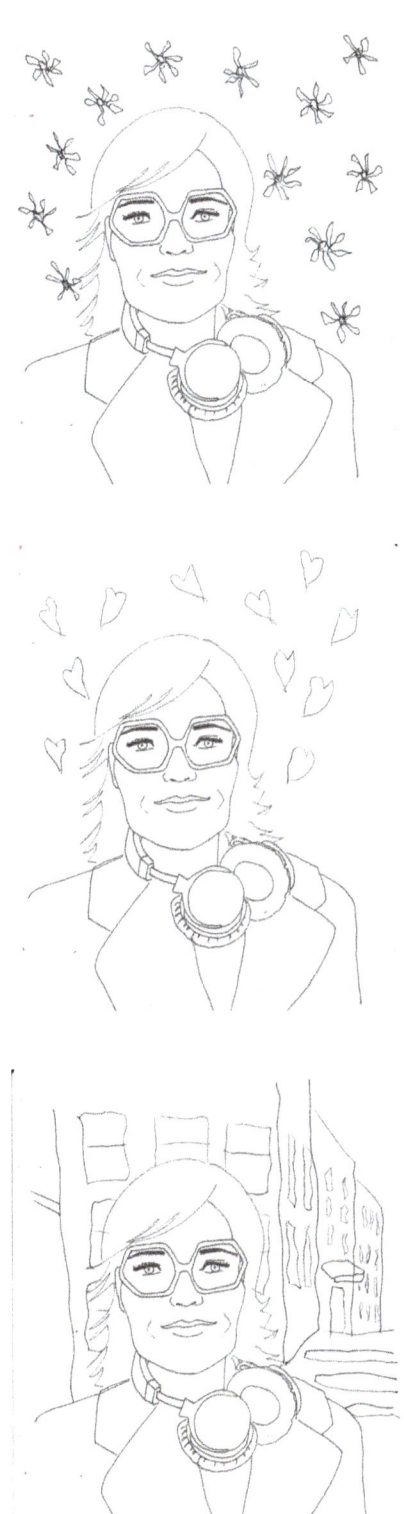

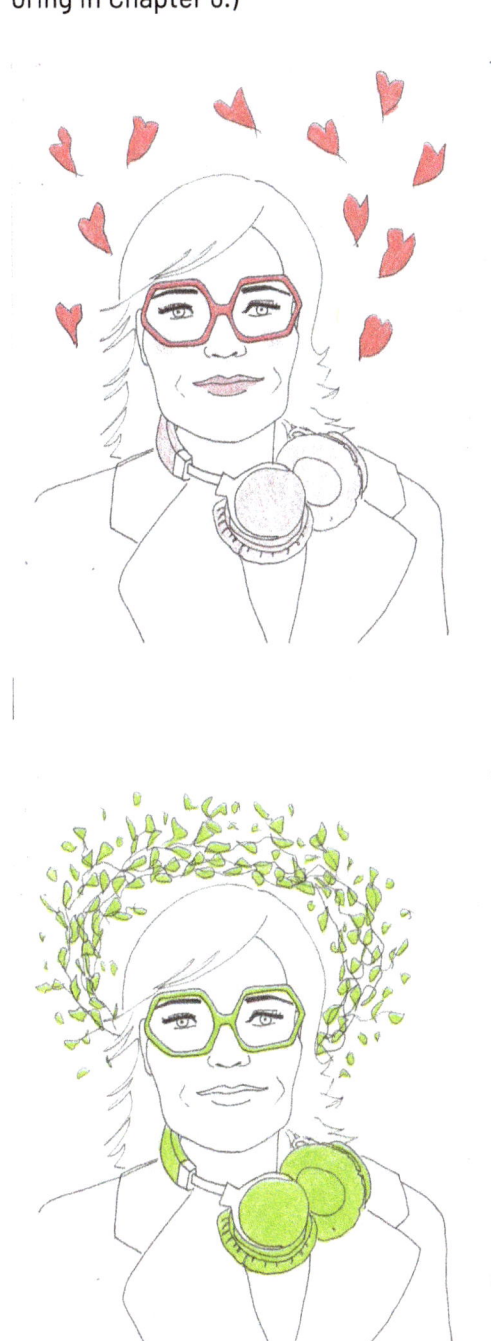

CHAPTER 2

Wreck Your Drawing With an Eraser

Start by making a drawing from life, imagination, or a reference picture

Don't spend too much time drawing details, as these will likely be lost in the erasing process.

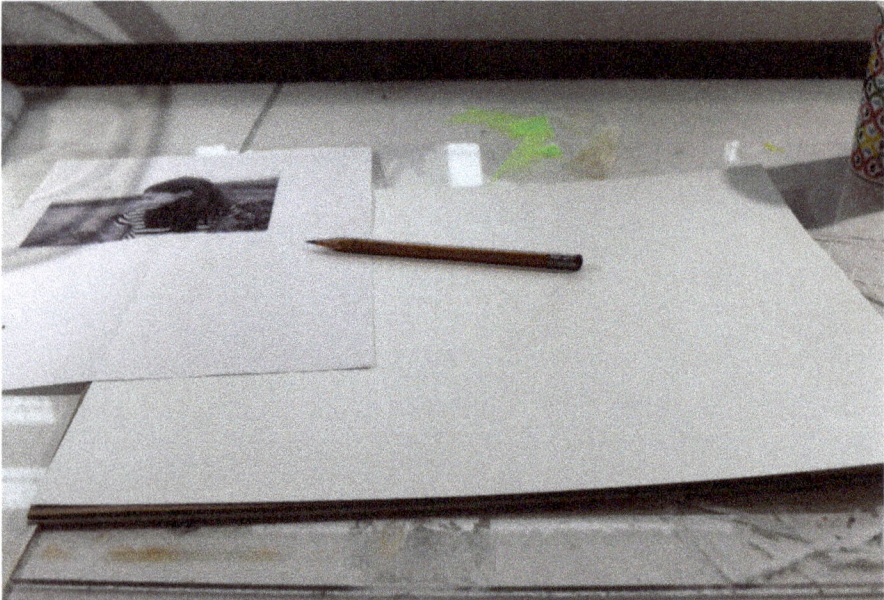

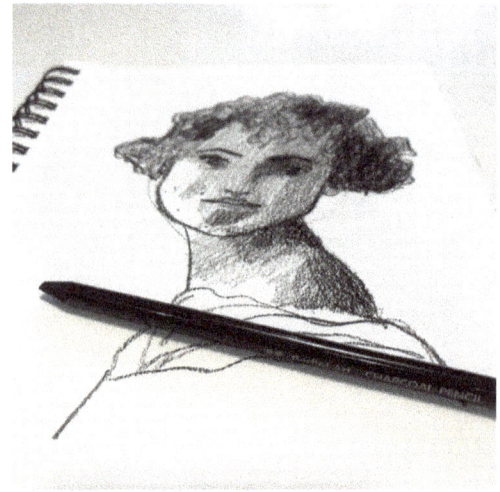

You will need

- **Paper.** Choose mixed media paper, bristol, Yupo paper, or any other type—just avoid printer paper. We'll be doing some vigorous erasing, and printer paper is too thin for this. Experimenting with different papers will help you achieve different results.
- **Drawing Media:** This can include pencils, charcoals, Conté sticks, or any other erasable tool.
- **Eraser:** I recommend using a white plastic eraser for this technique.
- **Reference Picture.** (if you're not working from life or imagination.)

Start by making a drawing. A higher-contrast drawing will be easier to work with later, as the erasing process will blend and smudge existing lines significantly.

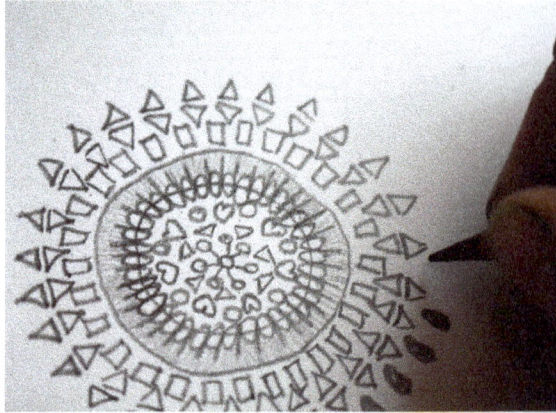

You can also experiment with geometric designs or *Mandalas for this technique.*

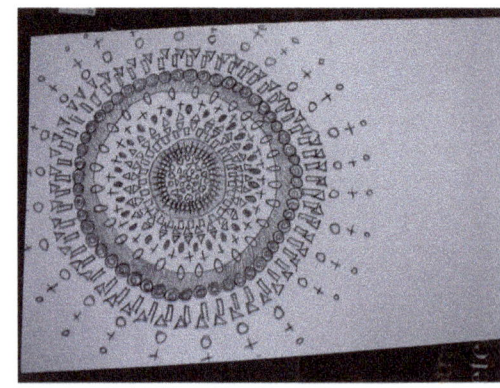

Once you are happy with your drawing, start erasing it.

Now is the time to erase! I find that white plastic erasers work best, but you can experiment with different types. You can also try different erasing techniques, such as back-and-forth strokes, lines going in the same direction, cross-hatching, or circular motions. This exercise encourages creativity and reduces attachment to the final result, making it easier to take artistic risks and experiment!

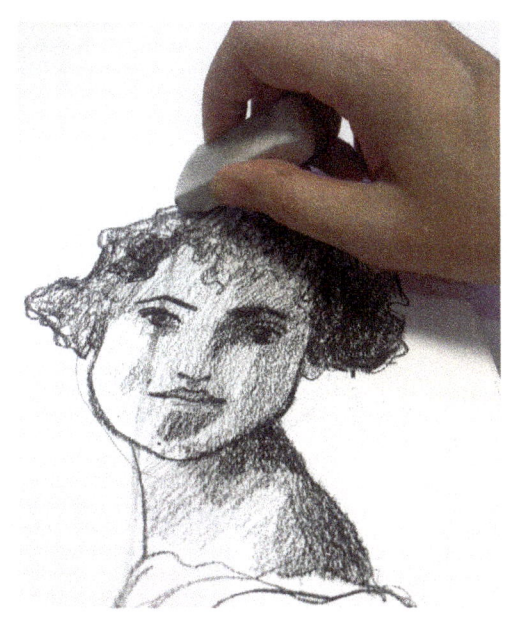

Here are some examples of what you can do with this technique:

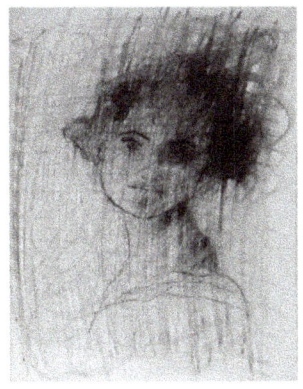

Portrait on mixed-media paper using charcoal and random erasing strokes.

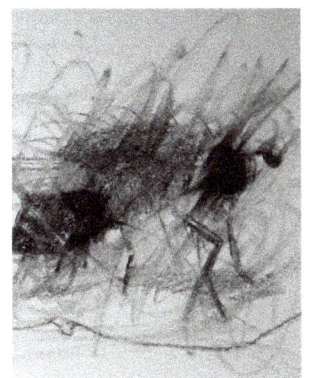

Drawing of an insect on mixed-media paper using charcoal and circular erasing strokes.

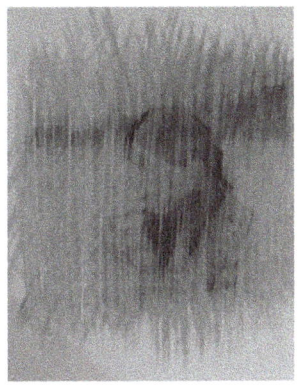

Example of portrait on Yupo paper with pencil and straight erasing strokes

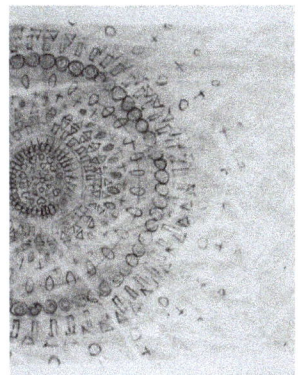

Example of geometric drawing on card paper using pencil and straight-line erasing in random directions.

Once your drawing and erasing is complete, you can clean up the borders by erasing neatly. For an even cleaner border, try lining the edges of your drawing with masking tape before erasing. On Yupo paper, try using a Magic Eraser and some dish soap to clean up the borders of the picture.

 TIP:
Use this technique to make greeting cards or postcards:

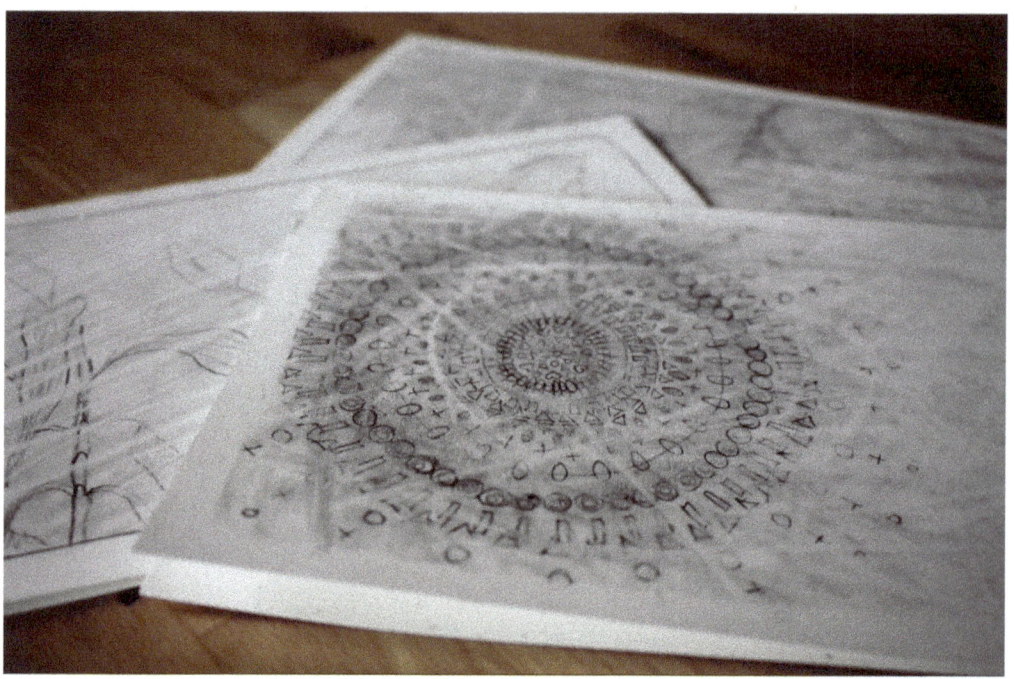

Example of greeting cards with erased drawings

CHAPTER 3

Simple Geometric Patterns & Zentangles

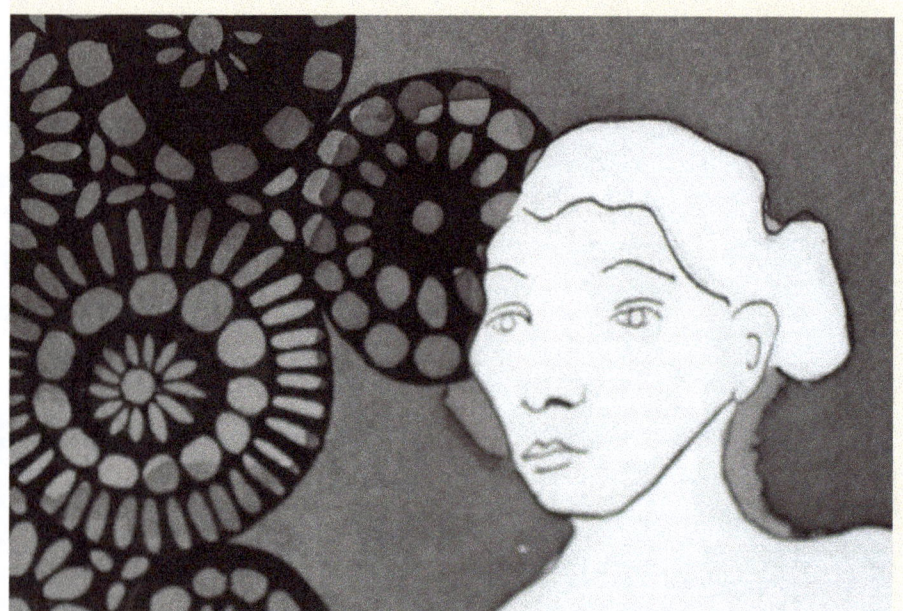

Incorporating patterns into an ink drawing

Whatever type of drawing I do, I often end up adding repeated patterns to my designs, getting lost in drawing patterns, and doodling or playing with Zentangles. You can use these techniques on their own or as a part of a larger project. You can draw on a small scale, like a post-card, or on a large scale on a canvas. You can use pencils, markers, or any other drawing tool and incorporate patterning into mixed media painting.

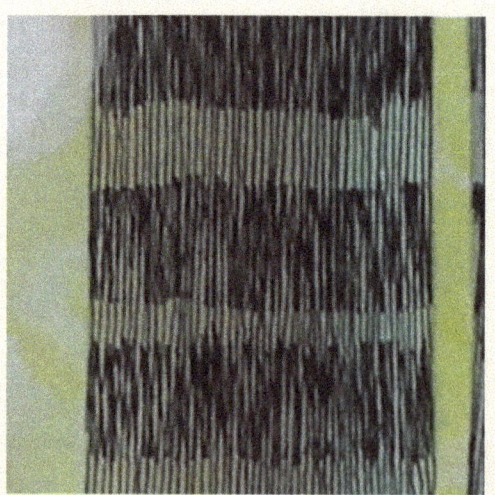

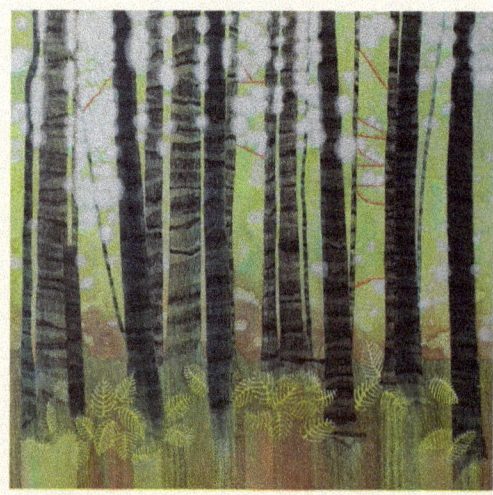

Examples of patterning in ink added to a large landscape painting on canvas

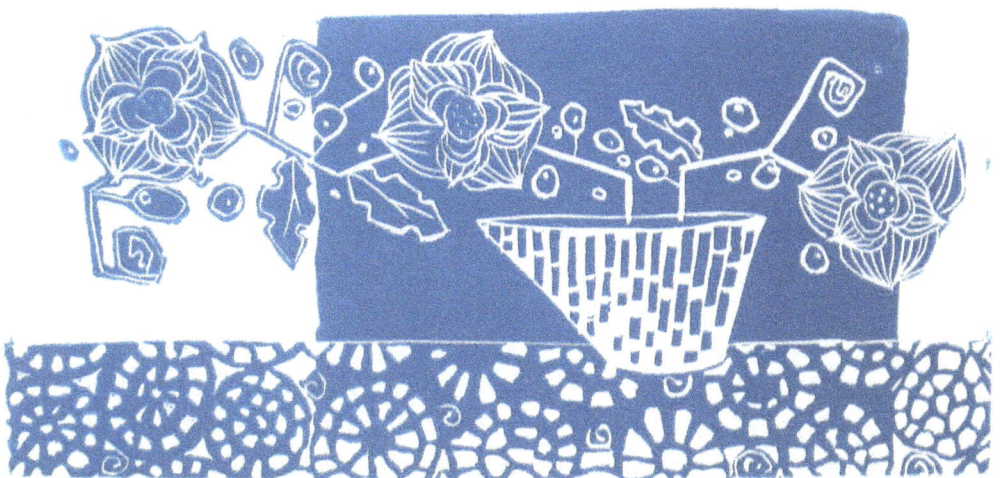

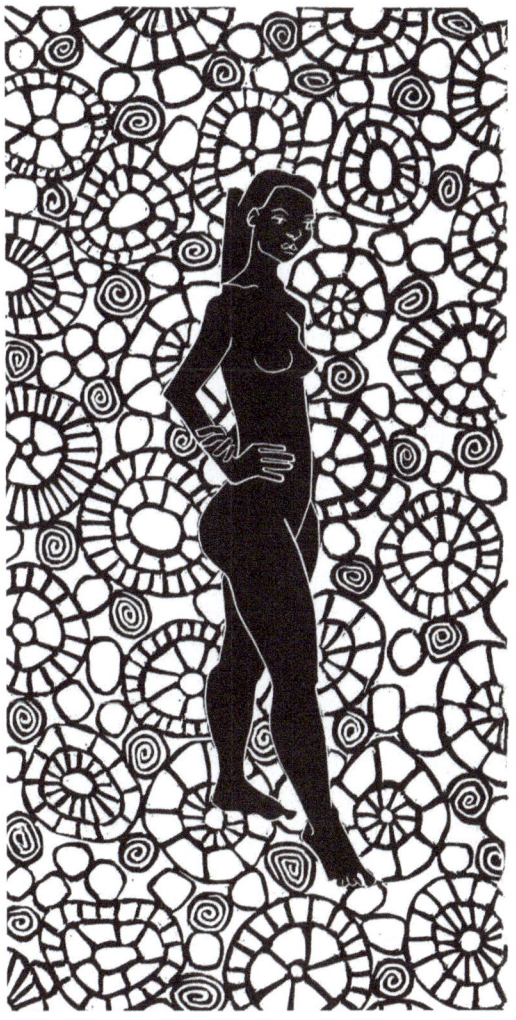

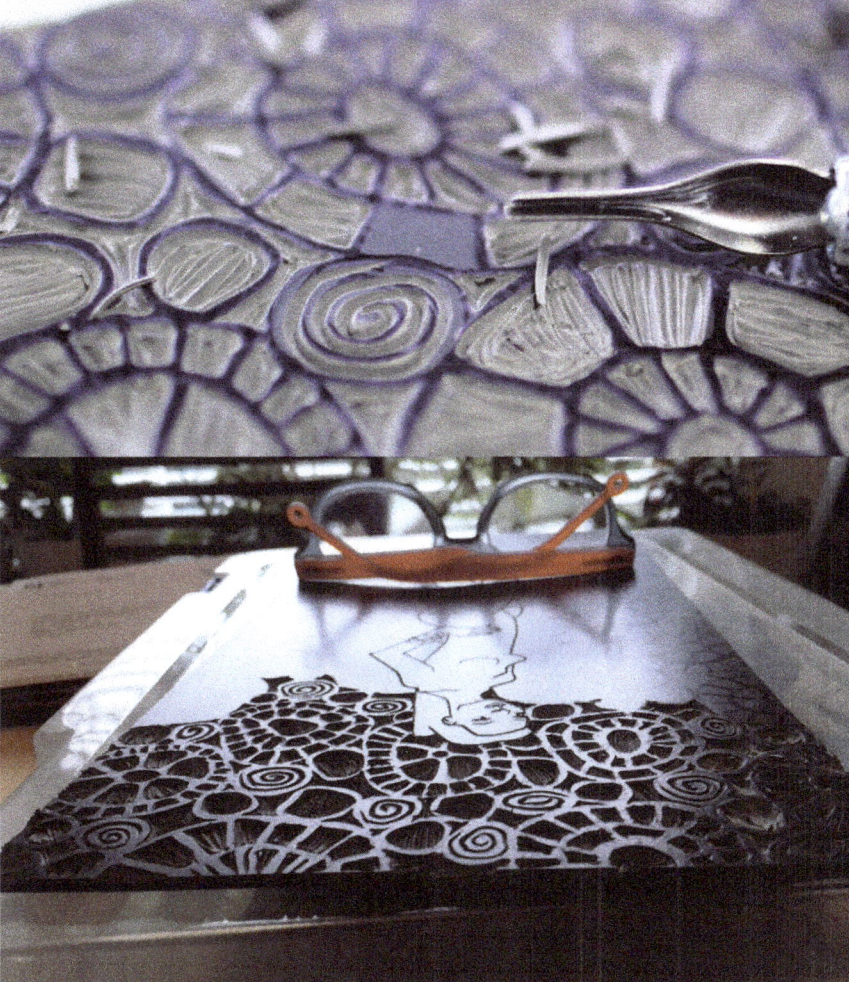

Examples of patterning on lino prints

Below are a few ideas to get you started with patterning and Zentangles:

Simple Mandalas

Amazing and complex designs can sometimes start with a few simple steps—and that's why I love mandalas!

To create a simple mandala, you will need
- Any thick paper (this can be watercolor paper, bristol paper, or mixed media paper)
- A fine drawing tool (this can be a fine liner or a fine-tip felt)

Other things you can experiment with:
- Black paper
- White gel pen
- Colored pencils
- Colored markers
- Watercolors
- Baby oil

Start by drawing a small circle somewhere on the page without tracing. Your mandala does not need to be perfectly circular; start with the smallest circle in the center, and see how it grows organically.

Because we will use colored pencils later on, draw your mandala directly with a fine line marker. Make sure your marker is resistant to mineral oil if you want to try smudging colored pencils with this technique in the next steps.

Start filling the area in and around the circle with patterns in a symmetrical or asymmetrical way. If you feel like drawing outside the lines, go for it! As you can see, I am building up the mandala from very simple shapes like circles, squares, stars, and triangles. The accumulation of these simple shapes forms a complex structure.

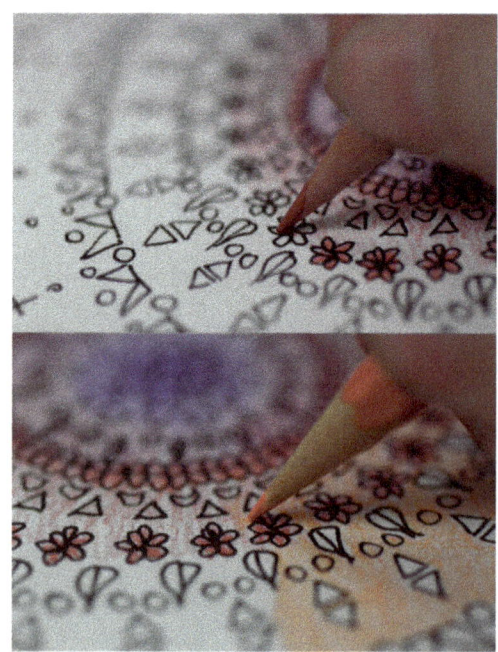

Once you are happy with your mandala drawing, you can begin coloring the drawn elements with various colored pencils. You can also color some of the background lightly against the more vivid details.

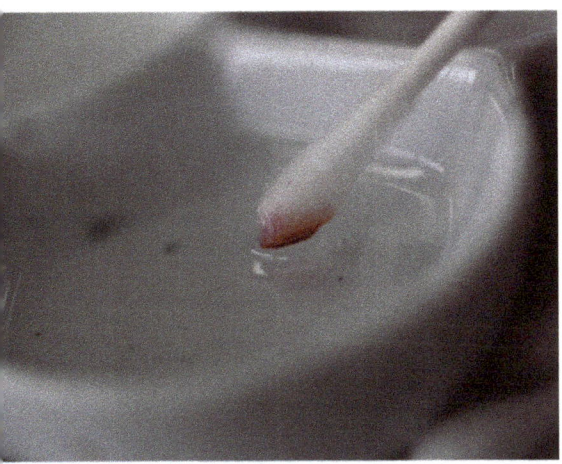

Once you are done coloring, if you wish, dip a Q-tip in mineral oil and lightly rub it against the paper to blend the colors.

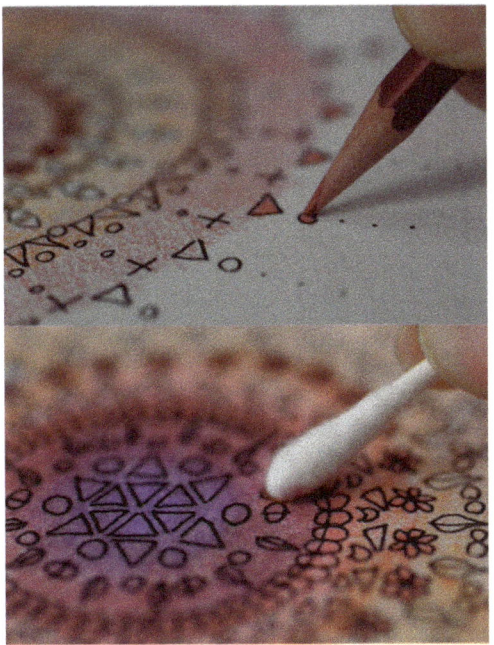

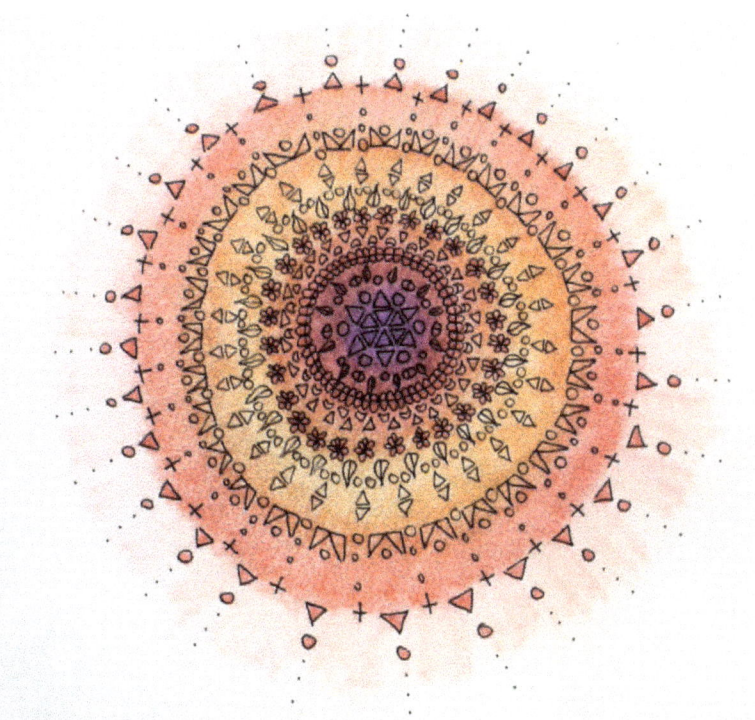

Example of mandala drawn with marker and colored pencils, blended with mineral oil.

💡 **TIP:**

Try drawing a mandala with white ink on black paper.

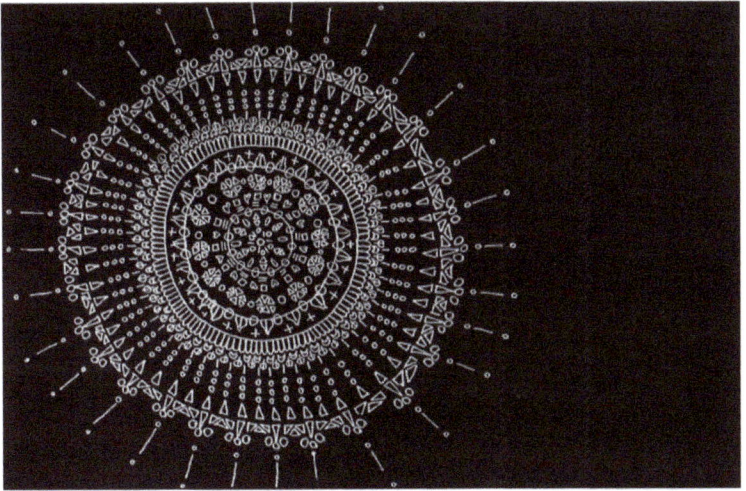

Adding Patterns to Sketches, Life Drawings, & Portraits

If you are going to a life-drawing class or like sketching from life or reference pictures, you can try adding some complexity to your drawings with repeating patterns.

Here are a few pattern ideas to try:

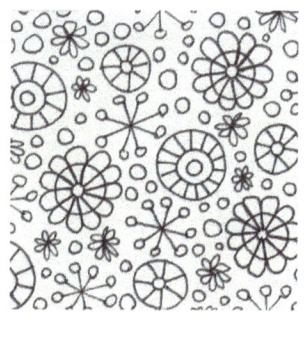
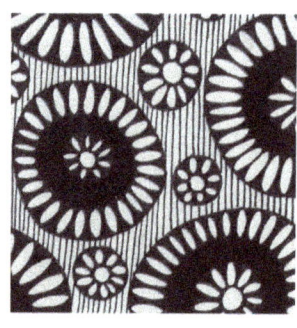
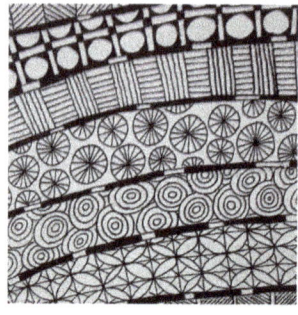
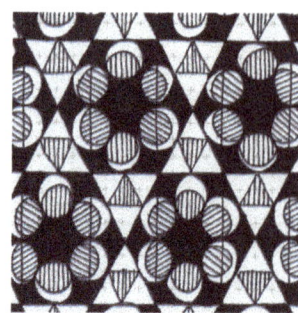

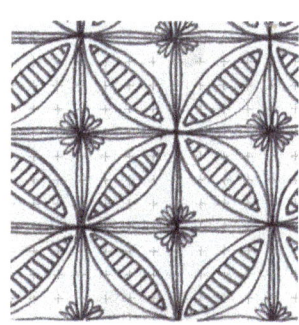
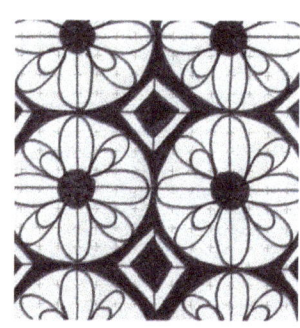
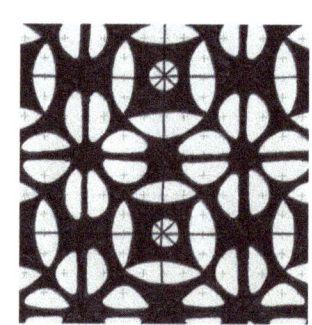
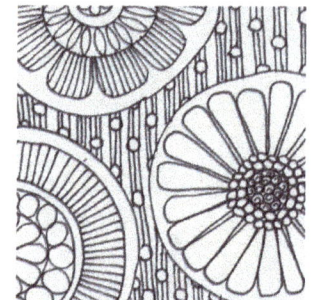

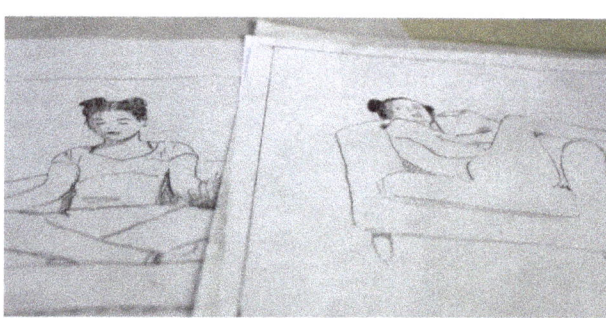
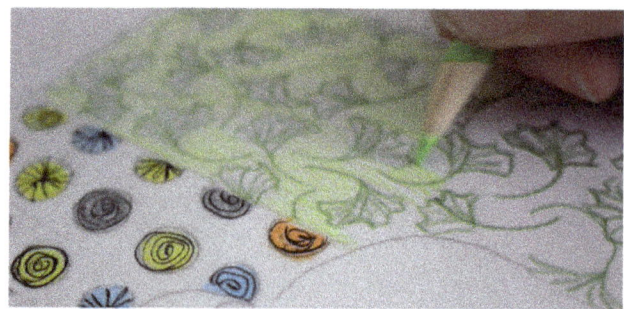

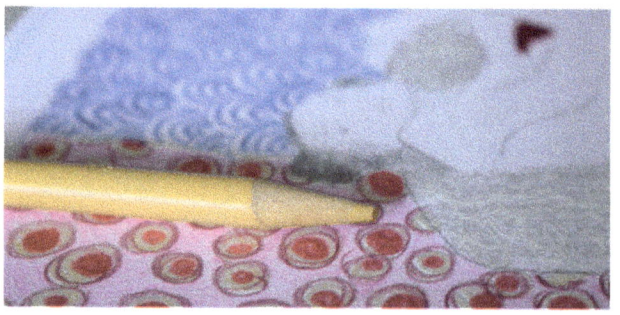
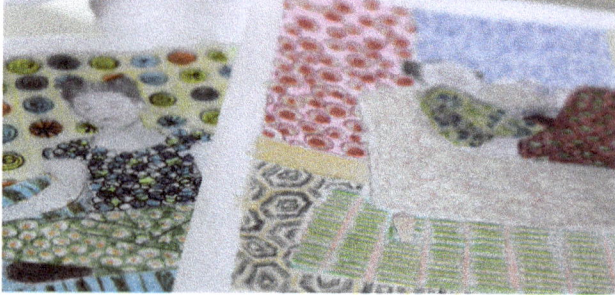

Examples of patterns added to sketches with colored pencils

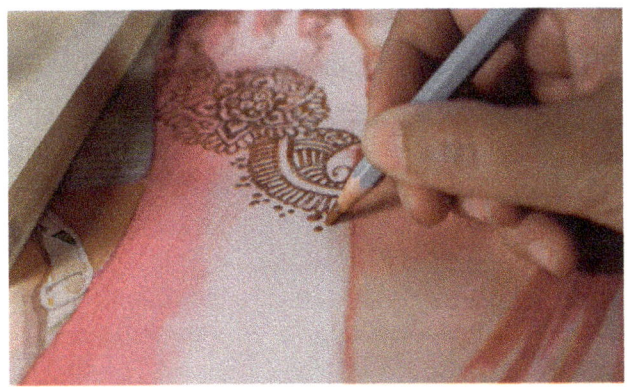
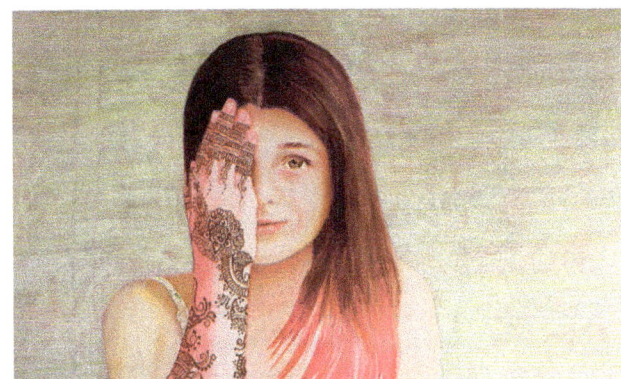

Example of a pattern added to a watercolor portrait

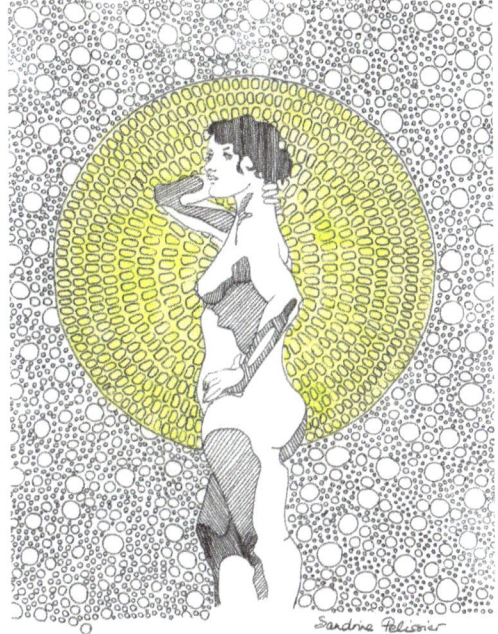

Example of patterns added to life drawings with ink

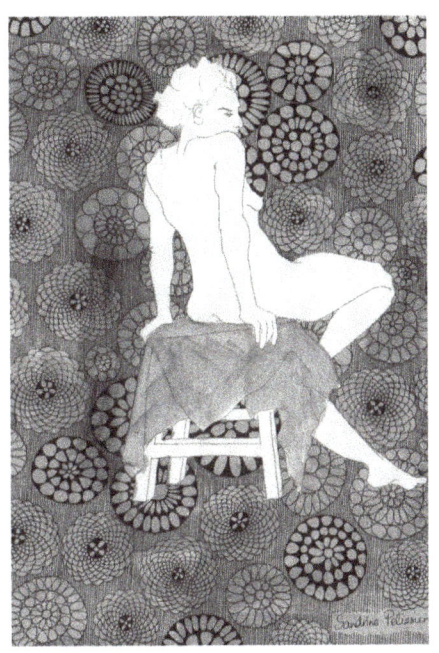

 TIP:

Build a library of patterns you like on memo cards or an online platform like Pinterest. Inspiration can come from looking at wallpaper, ceramic tiles, fabrics, nature, and so many more places.

You can use memo cards as a library of pattern ideas

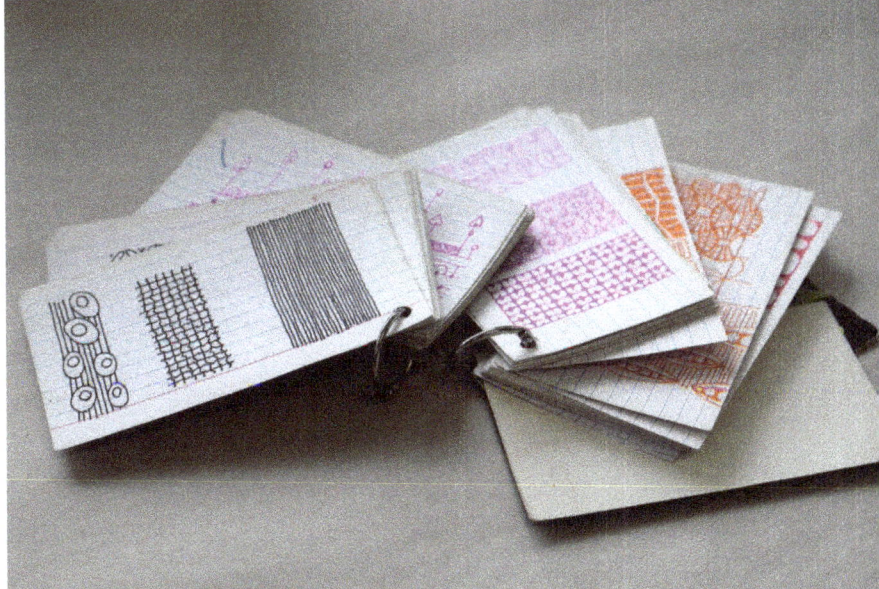

Yupo Postcard with Watercolor & Marker Doodles

For this exercise, you will need
- Postcard or watercolor paper
- Masking tape
- Watercolors
- A large brush
- Saran wrap or salt
- A fine liner
- A sponge (if you want to try the sponge texture technique)

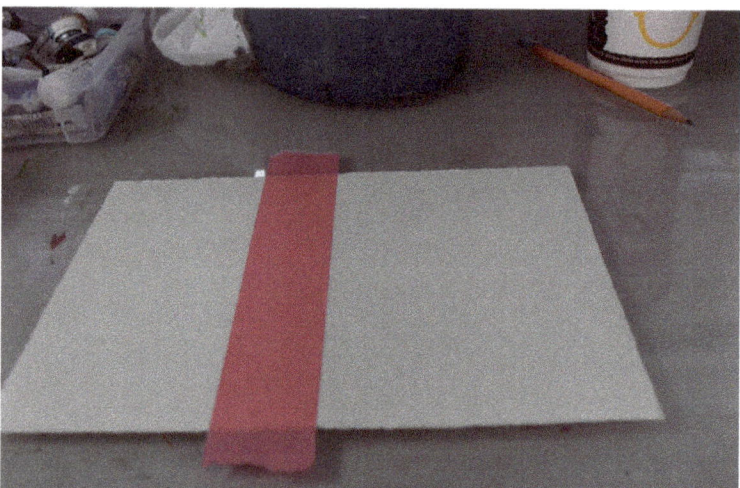

While working with postcards, you can try using masking tape to keep the edges of your design sharp and clean.

After taping, if you wish, the first step is to paint a textured background; in this exercise, we will use watercolors to do this. I recommend using two colors for the background: here, I will use some blue and yellow and some orange and red.

Apply the colors loosely on the paper with quite a bit of water, making sure the colors are not completely blending together.

Next, try adding textures to your creation. This can be done in many different ways:
- Apply Saran wrap or cling wrap on the wet surface and crinkle it in various places on the wet surface. Let it dry, then remove it to reveal the pattern created.
- Sprinkle some coarse salt on the wet surface. Let it dry, then brush the salt away to reveal the pattern created.
- Dip your sponge in a wash of a color of your choosing, then lightly dab the sponge onto your surface, wet or dry.

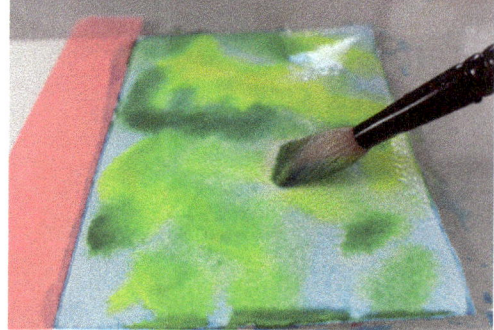

Example of loosely applying a mix of two watercolors with a brush.

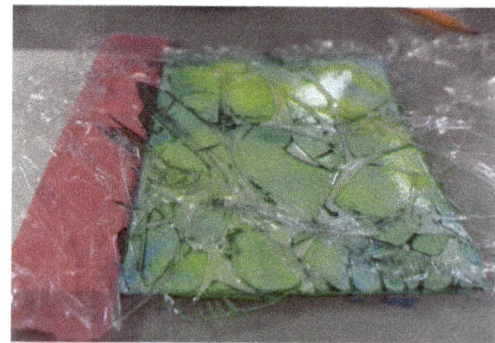

Example of adding texture using Saran wrap.

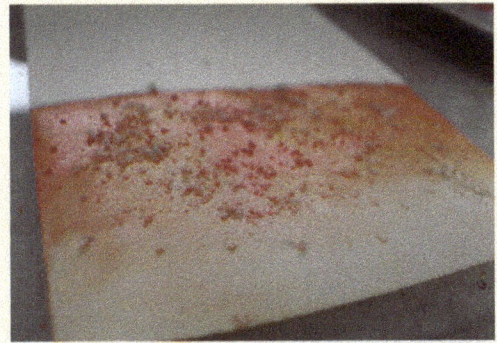

Example of adding texture with coarse salt sprinkled on a wet wash.

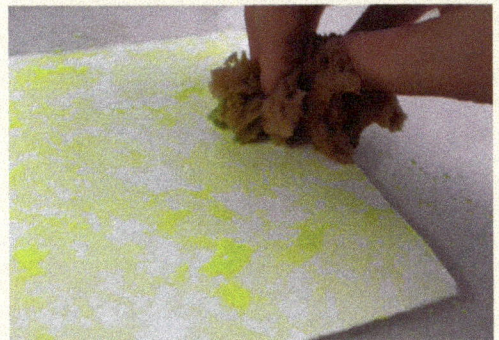

Example of using a sponge dipped in a watercolor wash to apply texture directly.

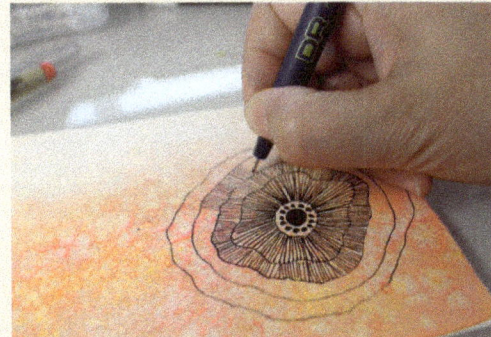

Once the texture added to your card is completely dry, you can start adding patterns or doodles with a fine liner.

Here are a few examples for inspiration:

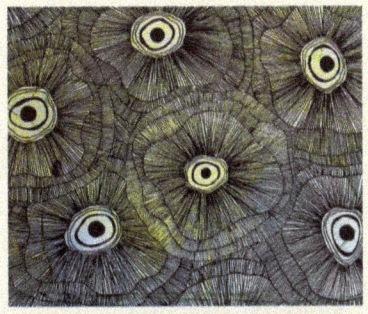
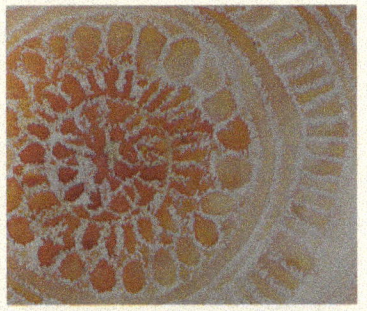
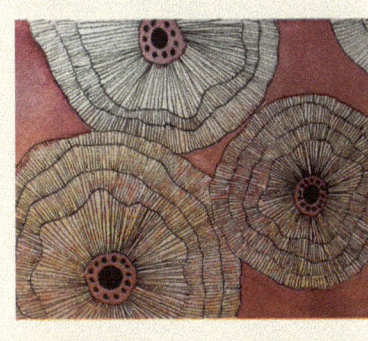
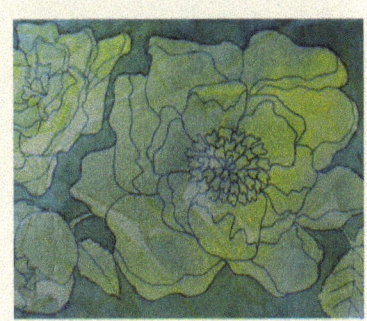
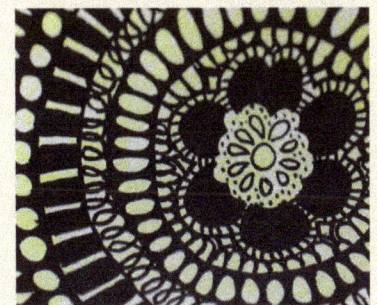
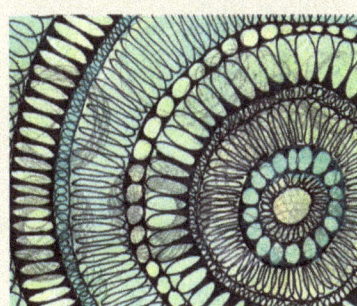

CHAPTER 4
Going Digital

Online Sketching Tools

There are many ways to get creative and make art. One of them is to do it all on your computer. You don't need to be a computer whiz: many online tools are easy to use and free!

One of my favorites to use is Super Sketchy, a collection of online art tools that can help you achieve amazing results.

Here are a few examples of drawings I made using Super Sketchy:

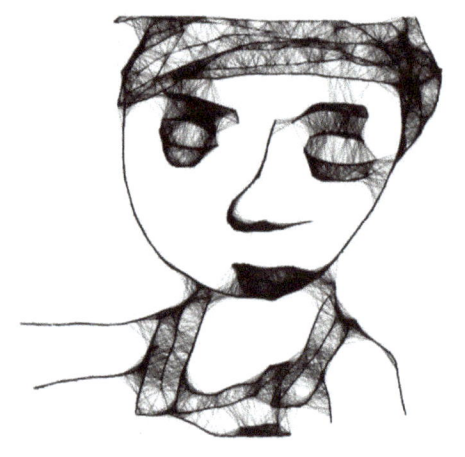

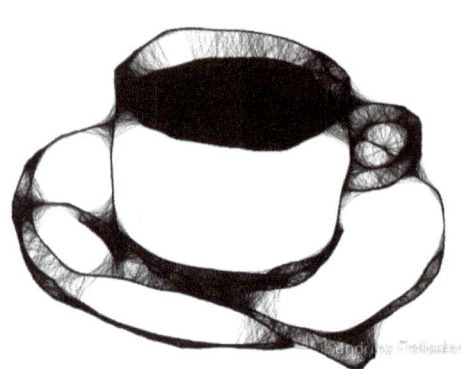

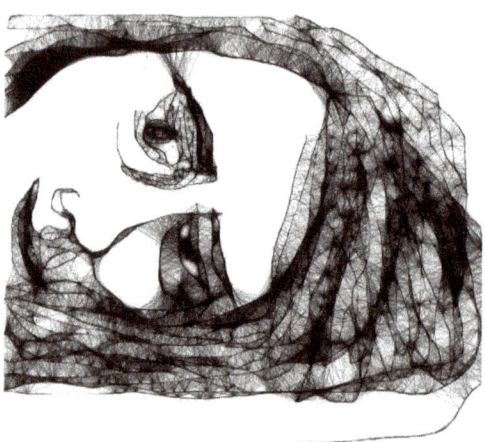

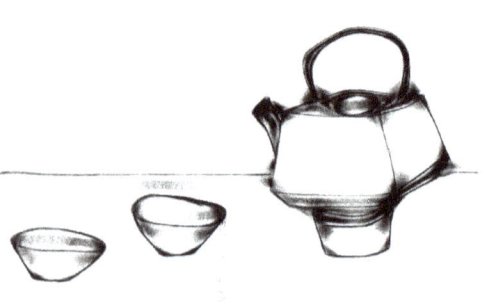

Sketching On an iPad

It can be fun to bring a tablet to a life-drawing class and use one of the many drawing apps available to draw a model.

Here are some examples of drawings made by my friend Anna duBois in a life-drawing class on her iPad:

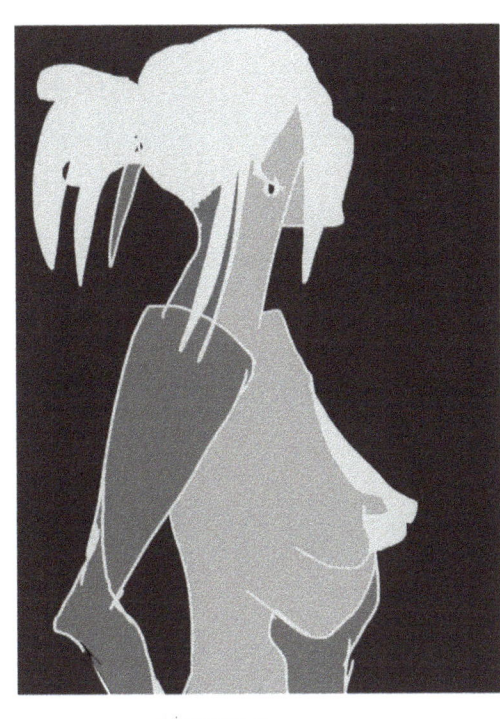

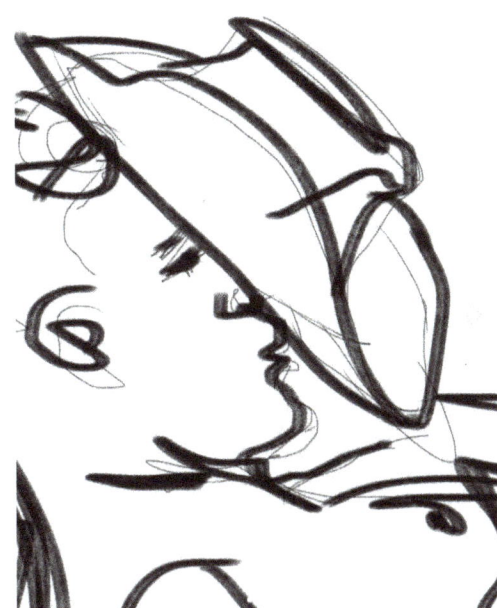

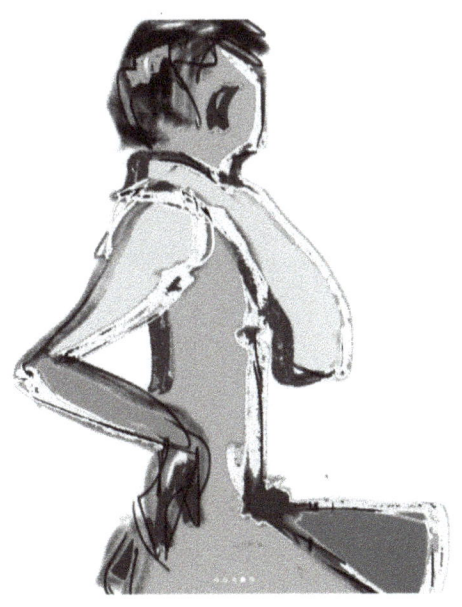

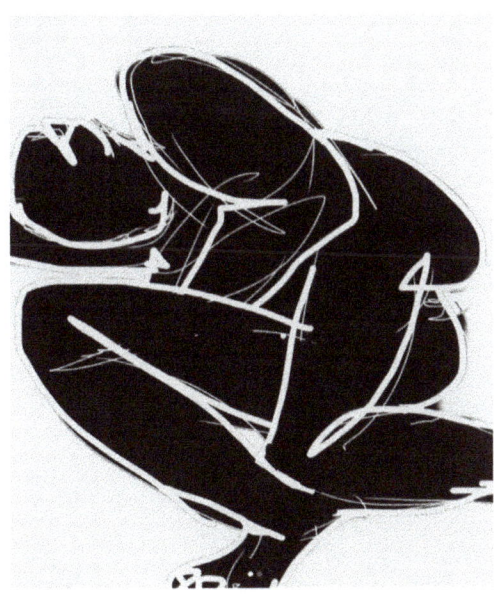

TIP:
If you aren't able to attend a life-drawing class, try drawing what you see on TV.
It can be fun to draw characters in a series or participants in a sporting event or
dance show.

CHAPTER 5

It's All About the Shade

I enjoy painting faces with ink while largely focusing on lighting and shade. Oftentimes, you are only painting the shade; the white of the paper acts as the light.

I did this exercise with India ink on bristol paper, but you can do it with acrylics or markers and achieve a similar effect.

If you want to draw from a reference image, search online for old black-and-white photos. It will be easier if the lighting is quite strong so the areas of shade are well defined.

For this exercise, you will need
- Paper: Bristol, watercolor, Yupo, or mixed-media paper
- India ink
- Brushes
- A water container and a palette (or several small cups) to make ink and water mixes

Next, mix a few washes of ink and water with different ratios of each to create a dark, medium, and light tone (at a minimum).

Observe your reference picture and try to simplify it in terms of broad areas of light, medium, and dark tones.

With a medium or large brush (depending on the size of your paper), start by painting the darkest areas and slowly work your way up to the lightest areas. The key here is to simplify: you don't want to get caught up in the details.

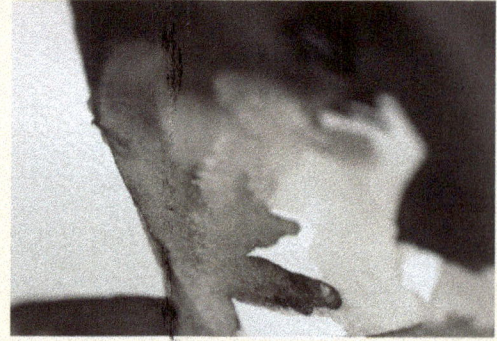

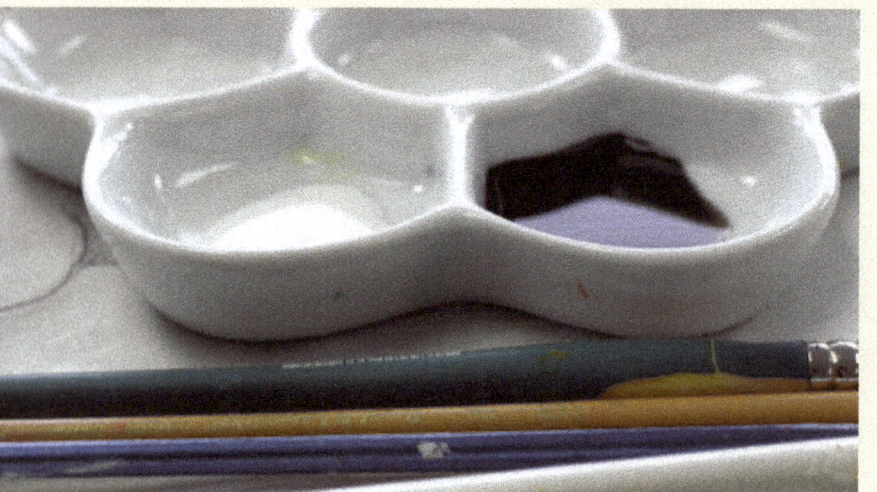

Start by finding a reference picture that inspires you, ideally one with a lot of contrast. I like working with portraits, but you can try this exercise with any subject.

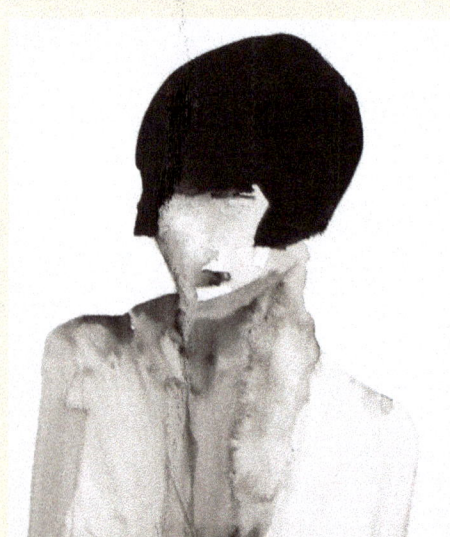

Don't try to be neat or precise. The object here is to work relatively quickly and avoid getting caught up in the details. Welcome happy accidents like the ink blooming into "unwanted" areas.

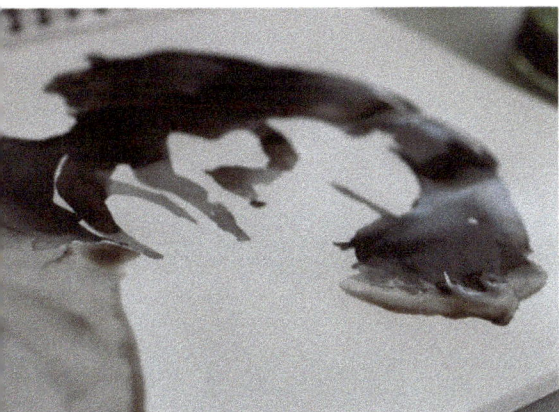

Focus only on light and shade.

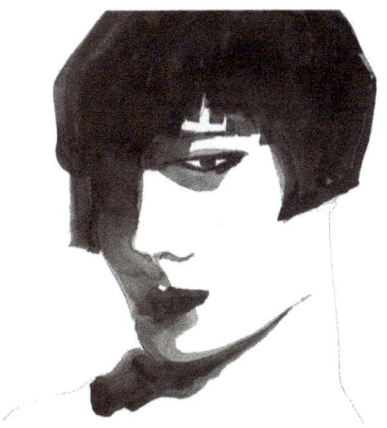

Example of details added with a fine brush.

I recommend working on more than one portrait at a time; this helps you work quickly and avoid overthinking about any one of them. At the end of the exercise, you can select the ones you like and discard the others.

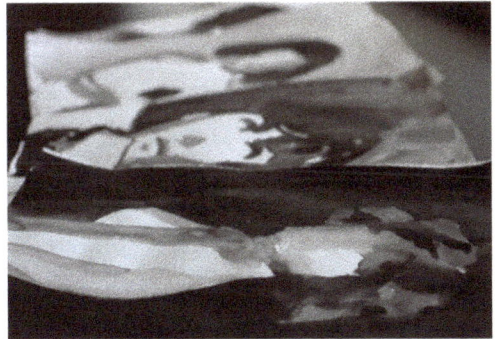

Example of working on a series at one time.

Now, you can add details with either a marker or a fine brush.

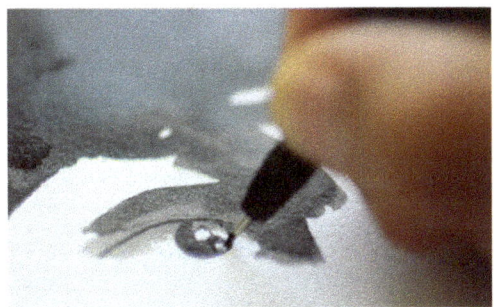

Example of eyes drawn with a marker.

The portraits you make in this style will not look perfect; they actually might look a bit odd, and the proportions will likely be a little bit off. But most importantly, you will be able to capture the energy of a drawing or a painting done intuitively. Happy accidents are welcome, and this is a great exercise to learn to loosen up while creating.

Here are a few examples of portraits done using this technique:

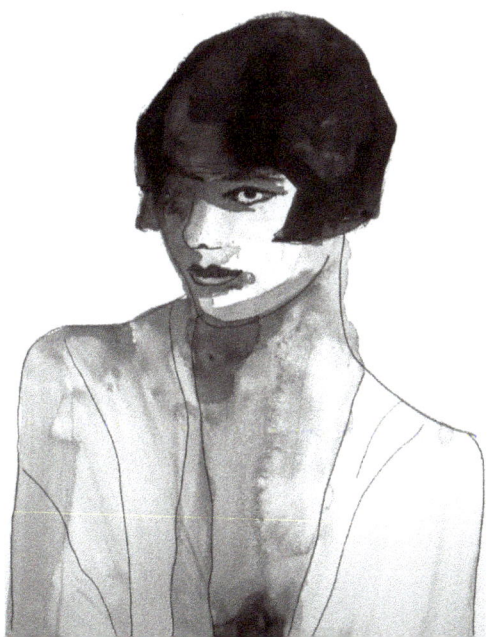

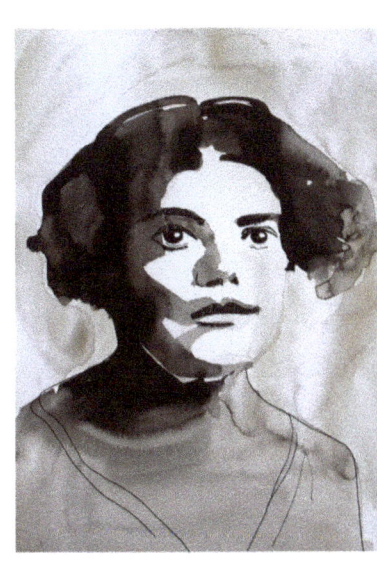

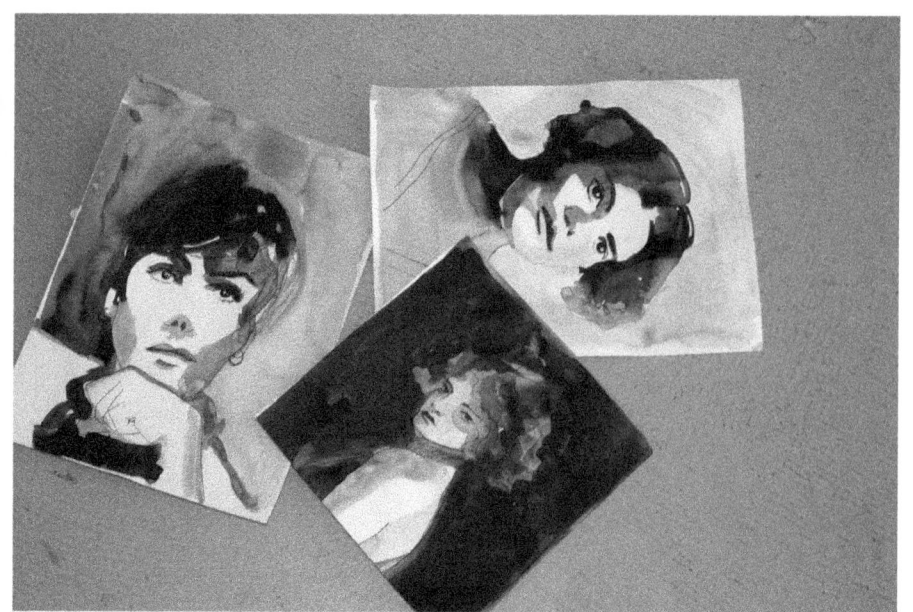

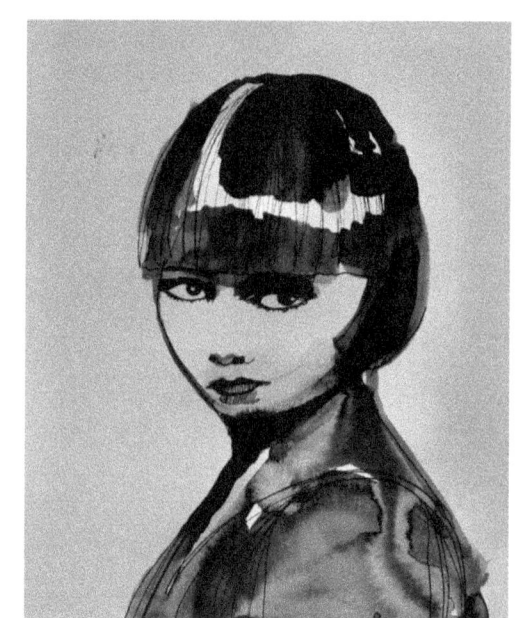

CHAPTER 6
Selective
Coloring

Selective coloring is a great technique to draw attention to one area of your drawing.

This technique involves leaving most of your drawing in black and white or monochrome and adding a touch of bright color in a selected area or a few areas.

For this exercise, you will need

- Mixed-media or watercolor paper (hot press so there is not too much texture and you can draw easily) or drawing paper (if you are going to use only colored pencils)
- Waterproof marker (if you are going to use water), marker, or pencil
- Graphite pencil and eraser
- Inktense crayons, watercolor pencils, watercolors, or felt-tip markers

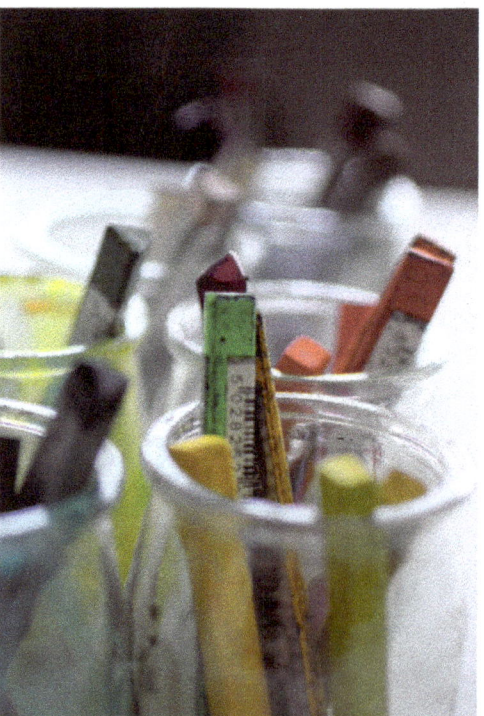

Inktense crayons are a bit like watercolor pencils: their color becomes more in-

tense once brushed over with water. You can use any medium that will give you a bright color like watercolor paints, watercolor pencils, oil pastels, or felt pens.

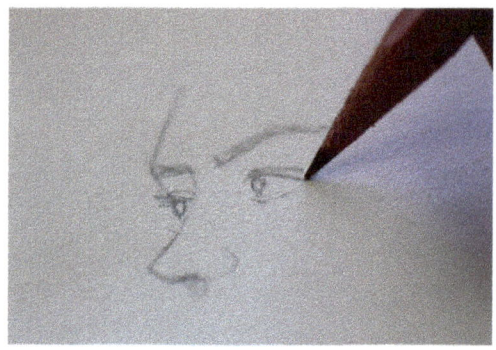

Start by deciding what you want to draw and what part of your drawing will be highlighted with color.

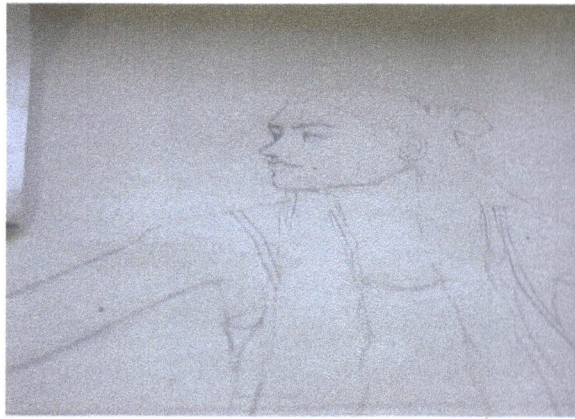

Here, I worked from a reference image of my daughter and did a quick outline with a graphite pencil.

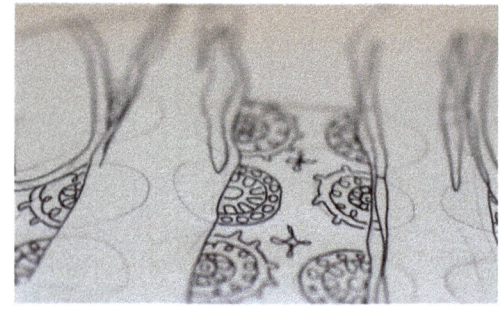

Although they do not exist in the original image, I decided to add patterns to her shirt to create more interesting detail.

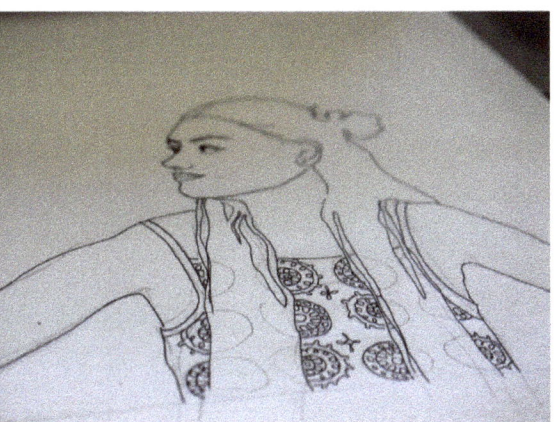

Once you are happy with your drawing, go over the lines with a waterproof marker so they stay sharp once water is introduced.

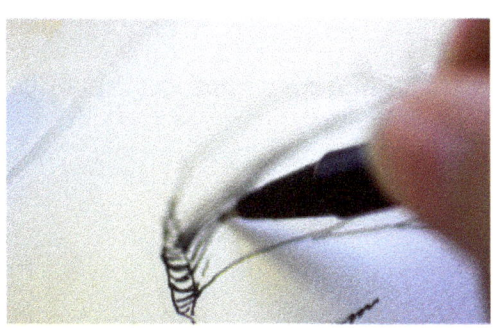

Because the hair is going to be the highlight of my drawing, I added some additional details in that area, as well.

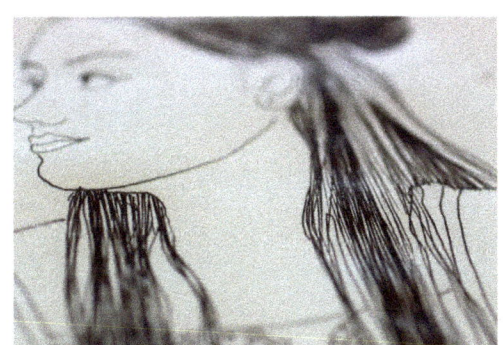

Now is the time to add color in the area you want to highlight!

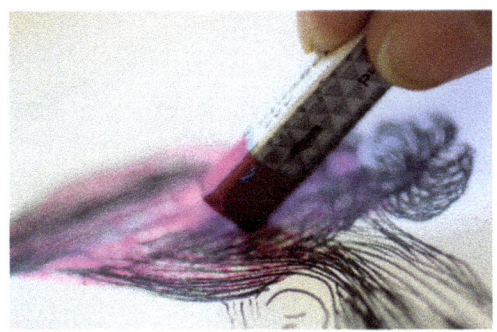

Here, I colored the hair with a bright pink Inktense stick.

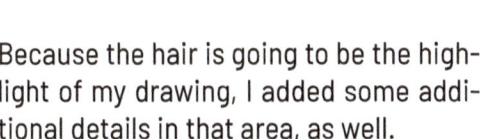

Here, I blended the Inktense stick with a brush dipped in water.

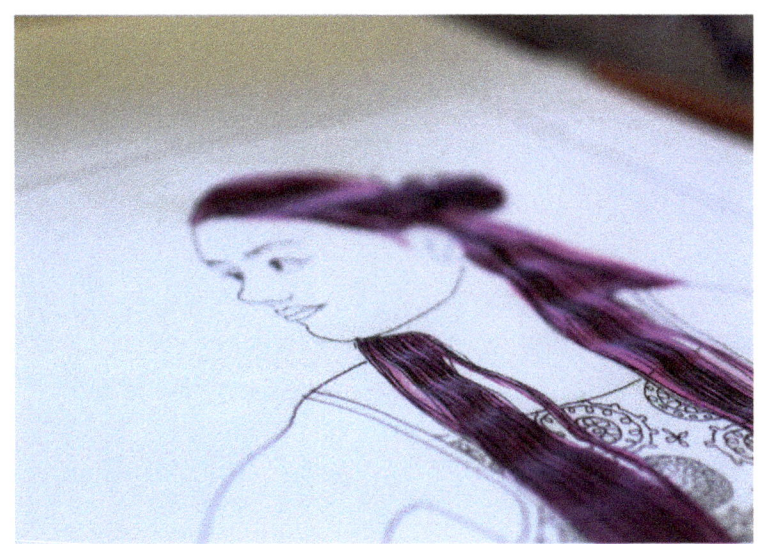

Then, let the paint dry.

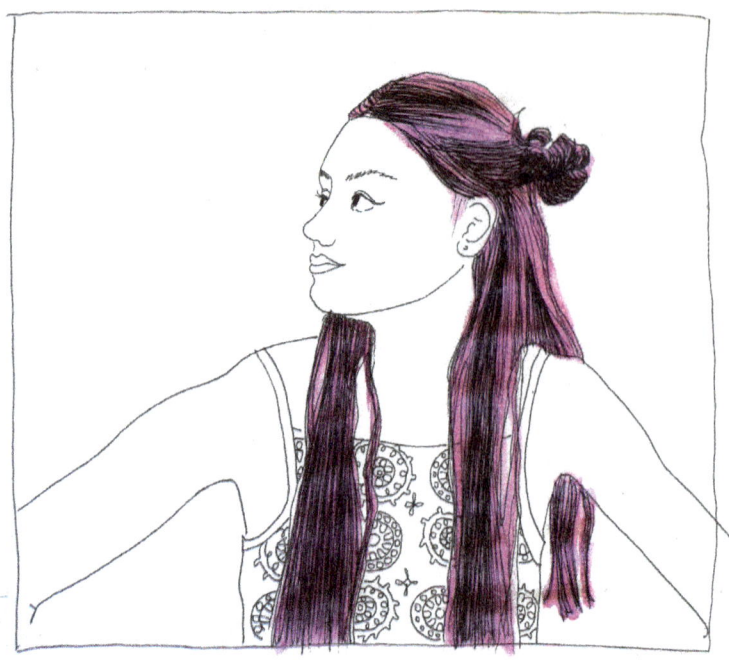

Example of a final drawing with a selective-coloring highlight.

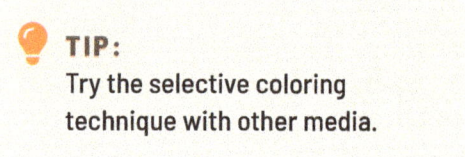

💡 **TIP:**
Try the selective coloring technique with other media.

Here are a few examples of selective coloring done with colored pencils on ink life drawings:

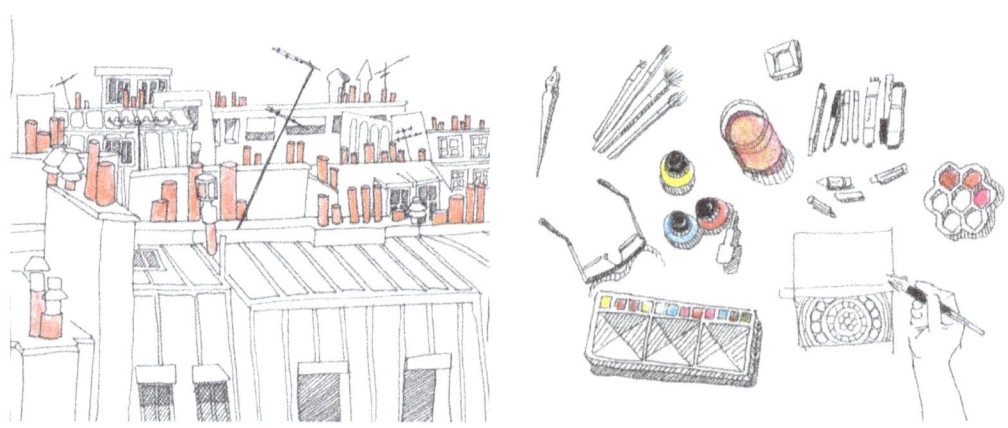

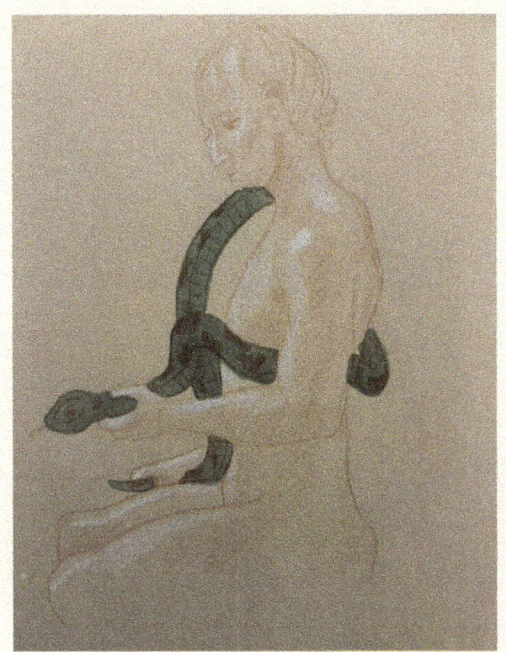
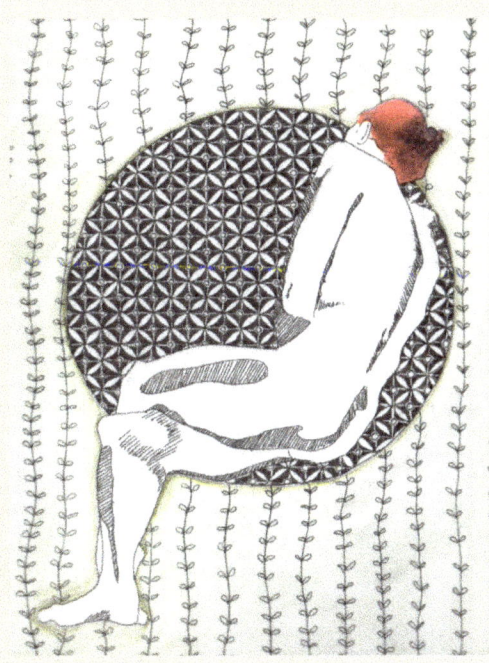

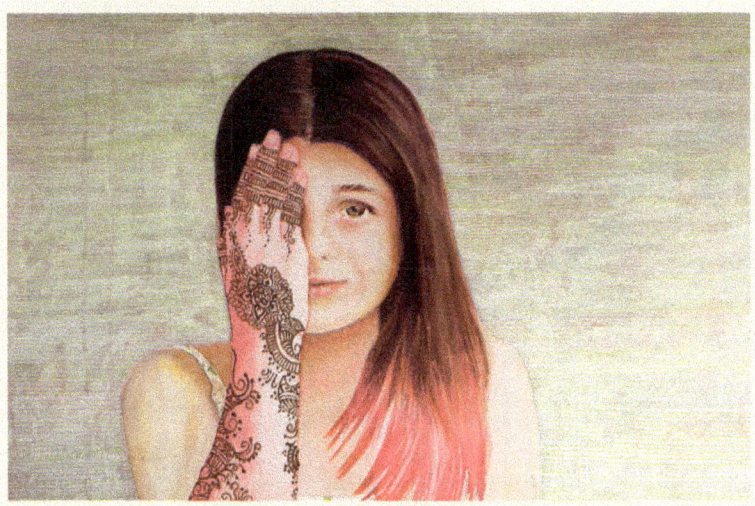

Examples of selective coloring in watercolor portraits.

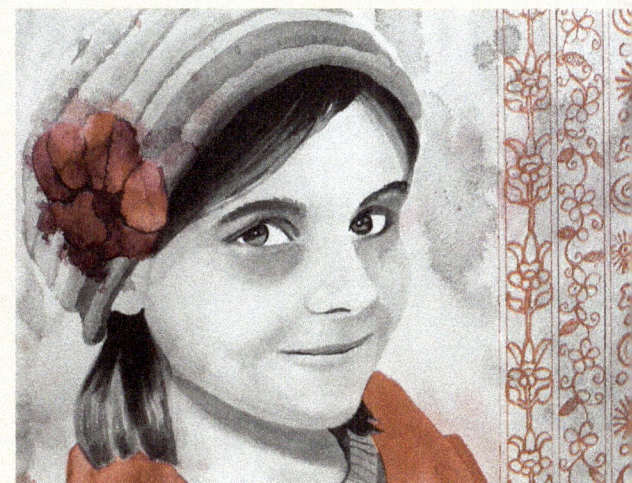

CHAPTER 7

Making Waterproof Paper

A Yupo Paper Alternative

Yupo paper is a wonderful surface to work on. Technically, Yupo paper is not paper at all: it is actually made of plastic. When the paint dries on Yupo paper, many different textures are formed. Also, if you make a mistake, you can simply take a wet cloth or tissue paper and wipe off the paint.

If you don't have access to Yupo paper, there are some ways to emulate its properties by making regular drawing paper water resistant.

This requires painting a layer of gel on top of your regular or watercolor paper with a soft brush so you don't risk damaging the paper. The gel, once dried, will make the paper water resistant.

You will need to let the paper dry thoroughly before using it.

For this exercise, you will need
- Regular drawing paper, watercolor paper, or bristol paper
- Liquid gel medium (I used gloss)
- A soft brush
- Paint (watercolor, markers, or oil pastels)

 TIP:
If you apply the medium over a graphite drawing, the drawing will remain visible while painting, but you won't be able to erase it.

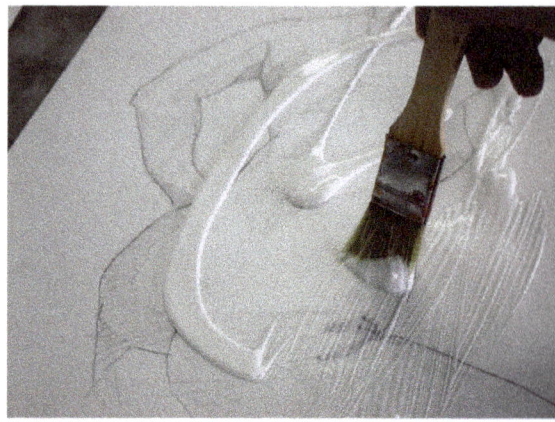

Example of applying a gel medium with a soft brush on a graphite drawing. The drawing will become sealed under the medium, and I will be able to lift off paint and try different techniques.

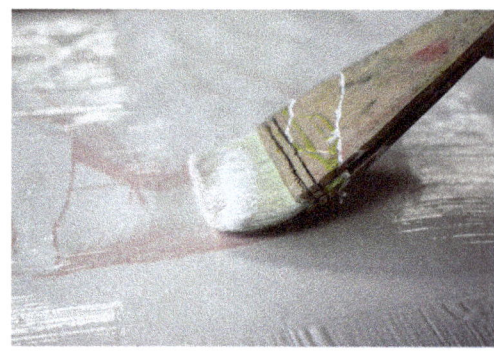

Example of brushing medium on oil pencil.

Once you have brushed the gel medium onto your paper and it has had enough time to dry, you can start painting with watercolor. If you don't like something, try lifting the paint with a wet brush or cloth.

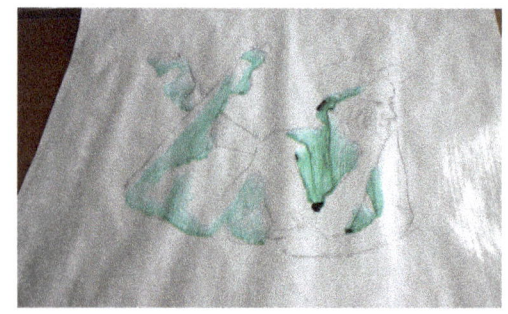

I found that I got the best results when I applied various watercolor paints and let them overlap and wash into one another.

Here, for example, I began with a layer of turquoise.

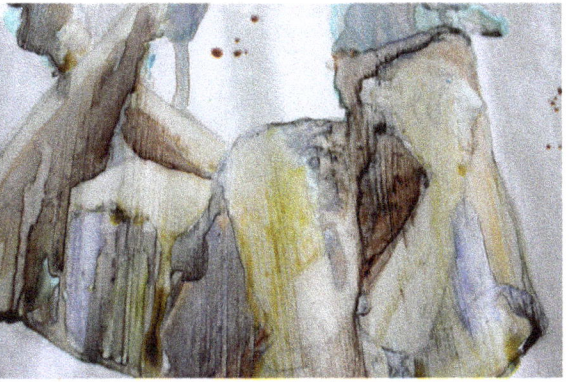

the grooves made by the brushstrokes on the gel medium.

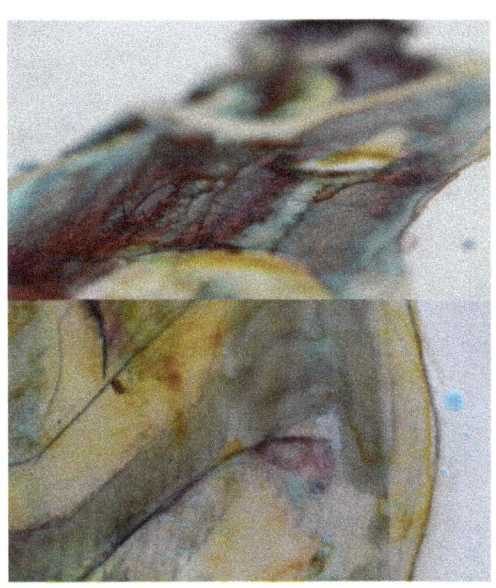

Additional examples of color layering.

I then followed this with layers of burnt sienna, ochre, red, and ultramarine. I also splashed a few paint drops onto the figure while painting. The paint will move on the paper and accumulate in

I encourage you to experiment with this technique. It works especially well to re-work life drawings made in class.

Here are some drawings that have been painted using this technique:

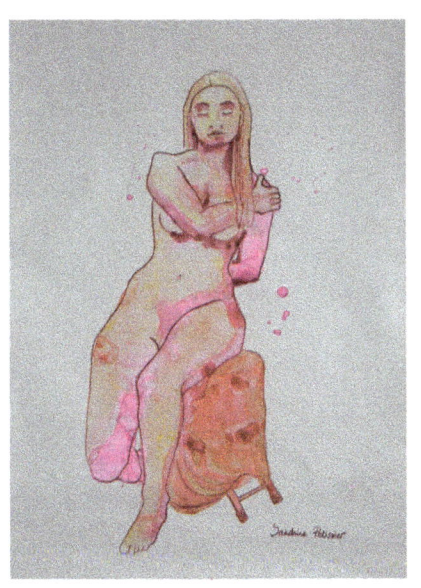
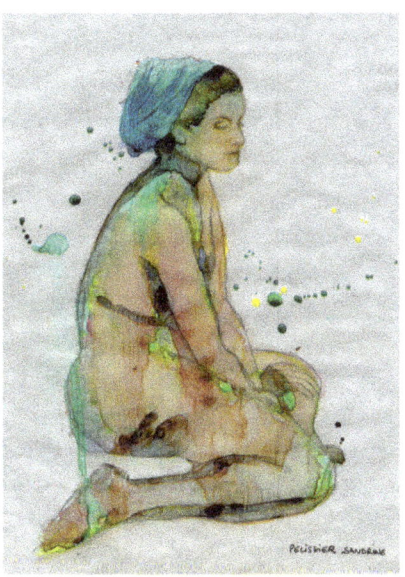
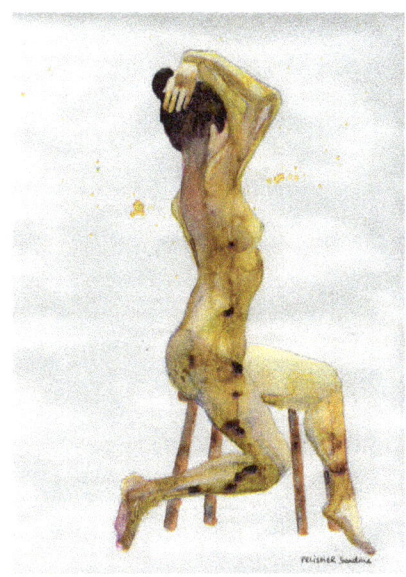

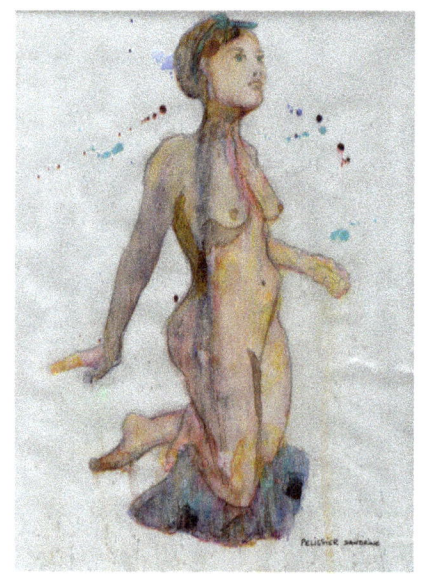
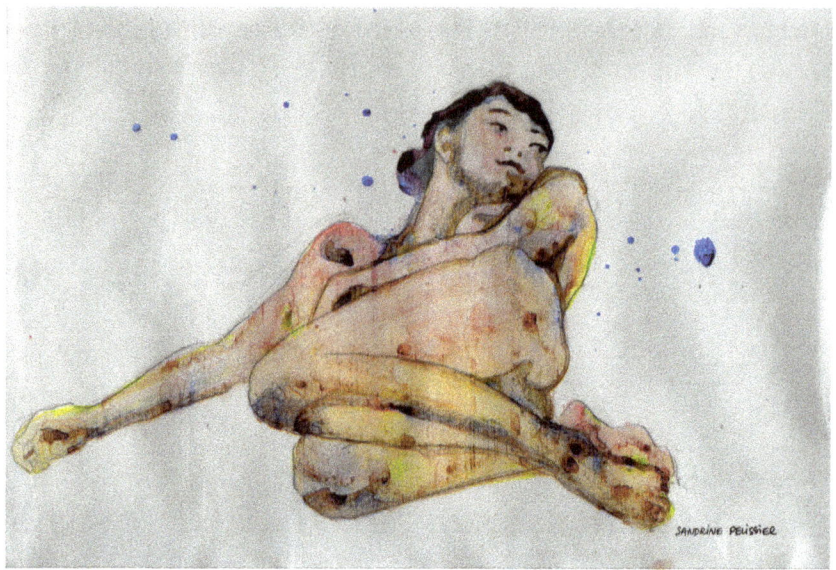
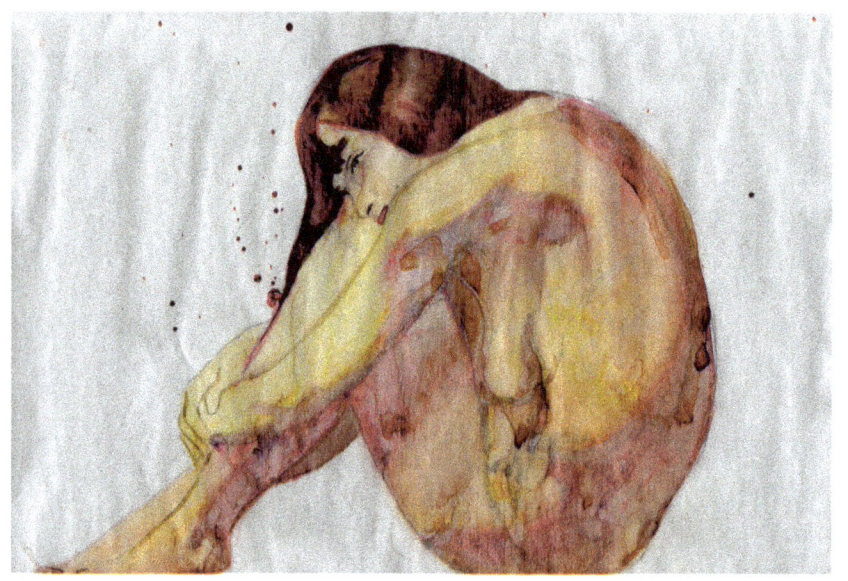
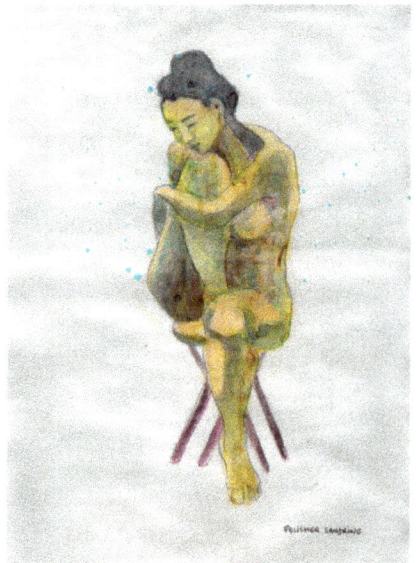
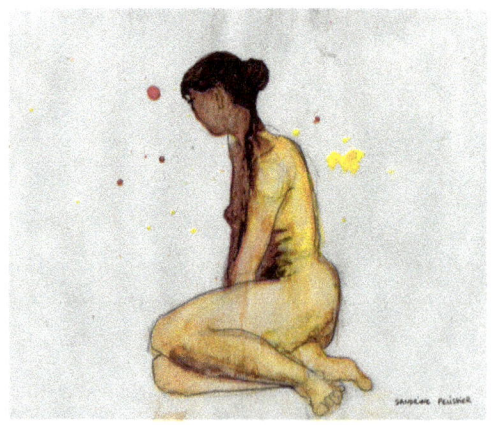
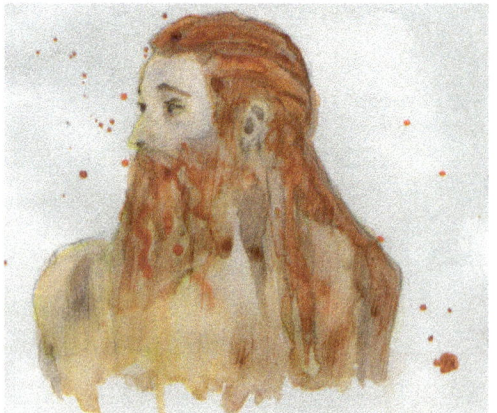

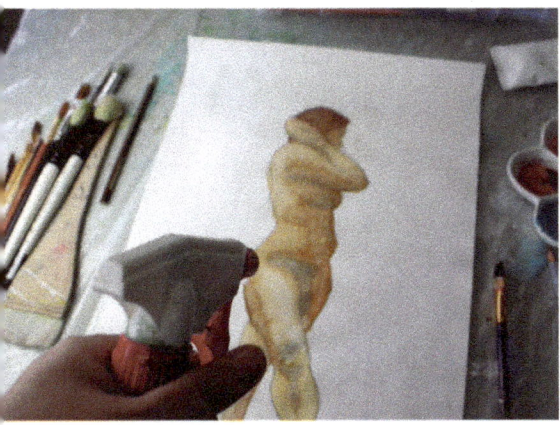

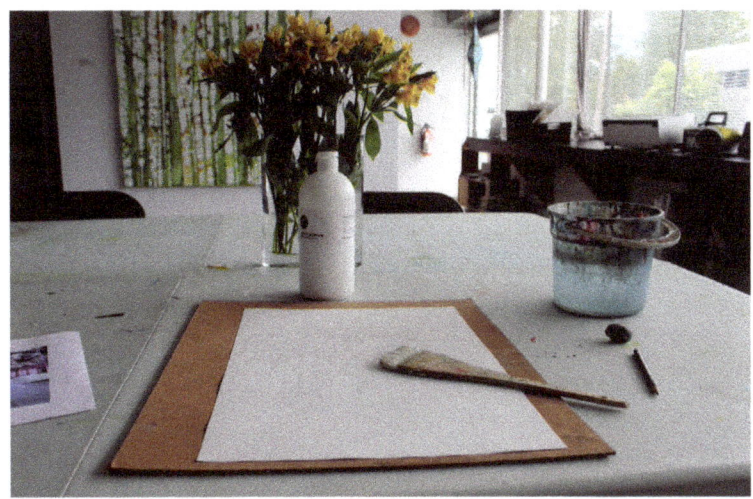

> **TIP:**
> Try experimenting with spraying the watercolor paint onto your page mixed with water.

For this exercise, I decided to draw daffodils from life. This is my setup.

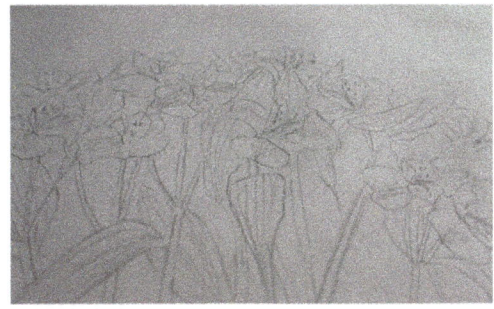

Painting a Still Life with Gel-Covered Paper

You will need
- Regular drawing paper, watercolor paper, or bristol paper (I used regular drawing paper)
- Liquid gel medium (I used gloss)
- A soft brush
- Paint or other drawing medium like watercolor, markers, or oil pastels

First, I drew an outline of the flowers and vase with pencil.

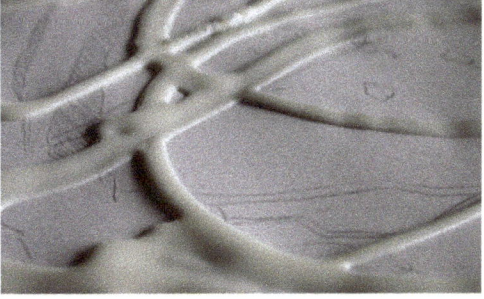

Once I was satisfied with my outline, I poured some of the gel medium (gloss) on the page.

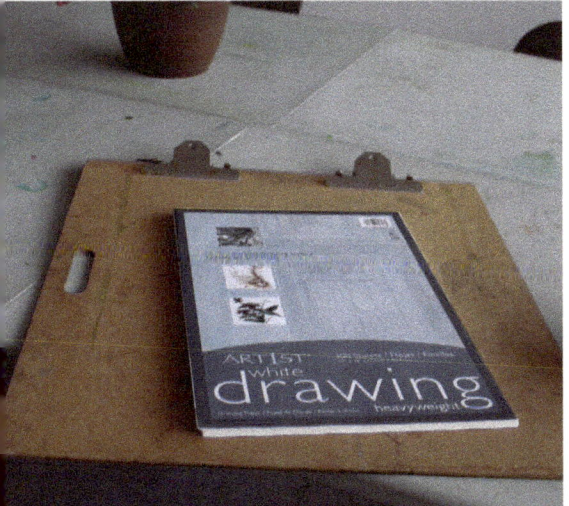

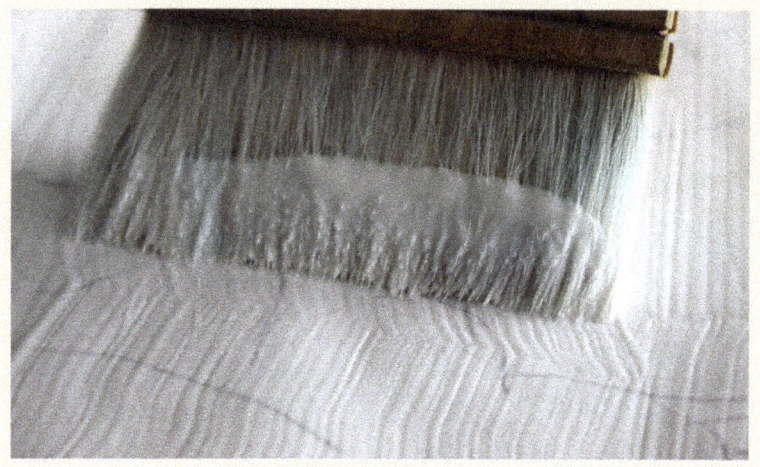

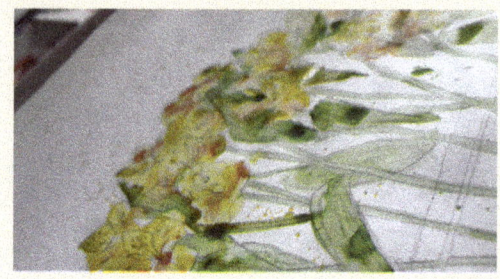

For this exercise, don't worry about being precise or staying within the lines; this medium and technique work well with a loose style. Remember: if you don't like something you did, you can remove it with a wet cloth.

Then, I spread it on the page with a large soft brush and let it dry.

You can also add some splashes of paint throughout the page, if you like that style.

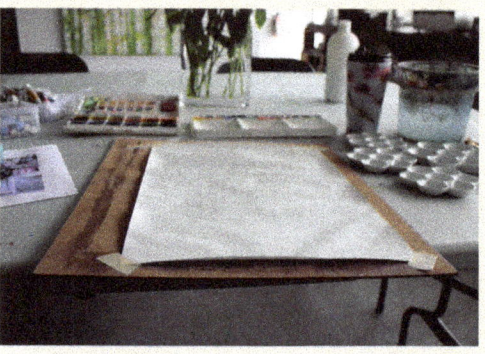

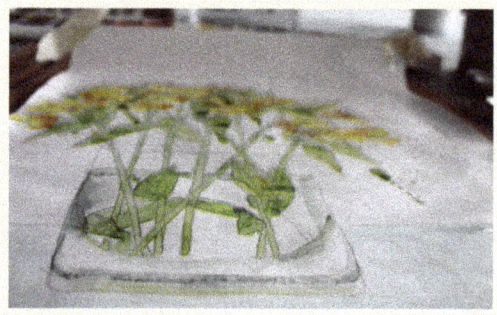

After your work dries, you might want to tape it to a board to avoid any movement while you work. You can then set up your watercolor paints.

Here is my finished painting.

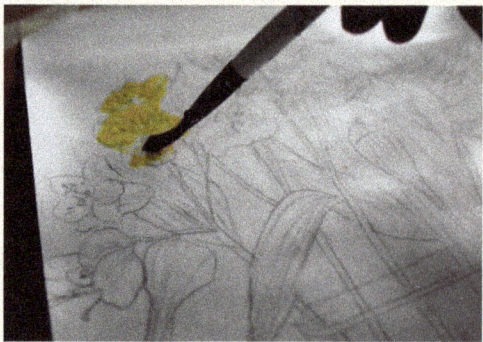

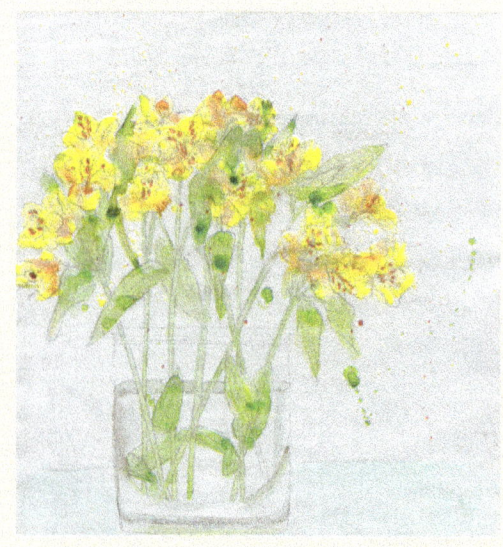

I decided to paint my daffodils using cadmium yellow, sap green, and crimson red.

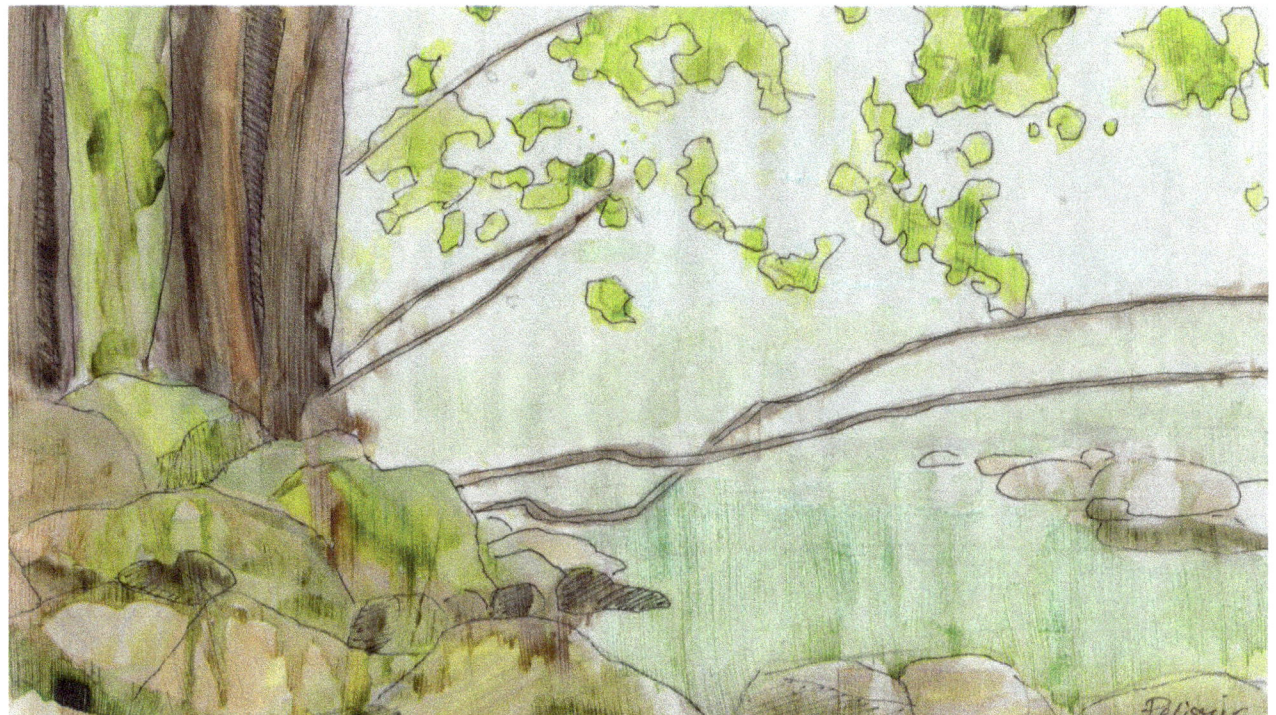

Example of a landscape painted with this technique.

CHAPTER 8

Comparing Different Media & Styles

This is a fun exercise for life drawings or any other type of artwork. It will help you explore different stylistic options and see what works best for you.

Here, we will create a few different versions of the same drawing using different media, exploring different styles. You can even think about your favorite artist and try a version of your drawing in their style.

The Original Drawing

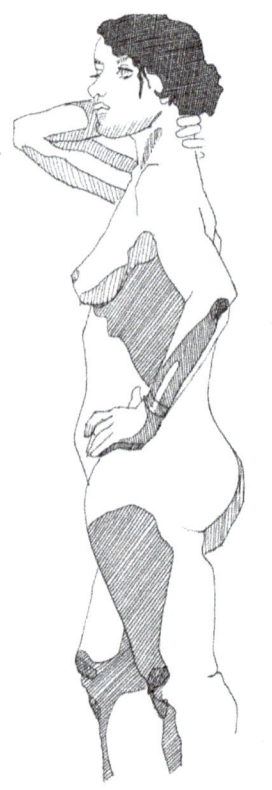

For this original drawing, I used graphite first, on mixed-media paper, to outline my figure. Then, I went over it with a black marker and erased the graphite outline underneath. I also used cross-hatching for the shaded areas.

From this initial drawing, you can create different variations with different media using the same base drawing. Here, I drew my original drawing on several sheets of drawing paper using a light box. You can also use the light from a window or use tracing paper.

You will need
• Your original drawing
• Drawing paper (multiple sheets)
• Painting brushes

Depending on what you would like to try, you might need
• Charcoal
• Watercolor paper
• Mixed media paper
• White acrylic paint
• Watercolor pencils
• Fine-line markers

Using Charcoal & White Acrylic Paint

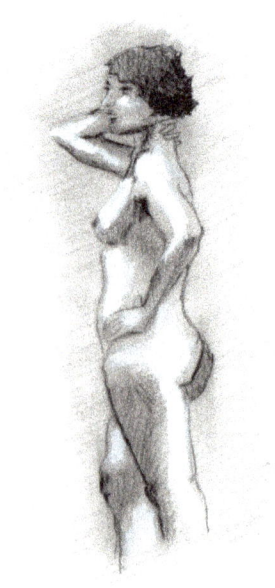

For this version, I used charcoal for the dark areas with an irregular cross-hatching pattern. I then smudged charcoal all over the white paper for the mid-tones and used white acrylic paint for the highlights.

Using Watercolor Pencils

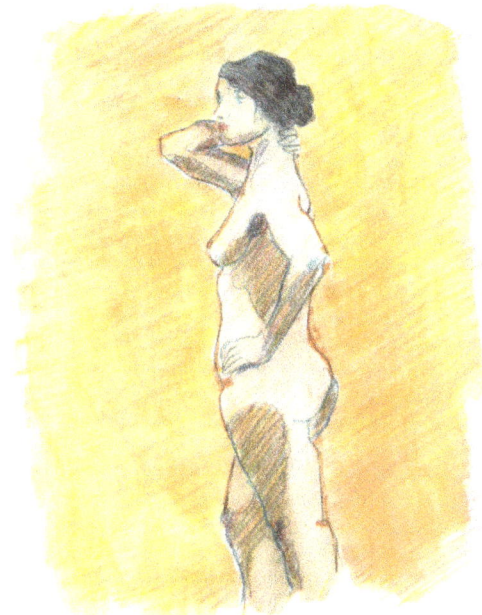

For this painting, I used watercolor paper and then mixed a few watercolor pencil colors (blue, yellow, orange, red, and black) before going over the painting with a wet brush.

Using Watercolor Washes & A Black Outline

Here, I also used watercolor paper. I began with an outline of the figure using a waterproof black marker (Sakura Pigma Micron) and then painted a light wash over the figure, adding a few red highlights using a wet-into-wet technique.

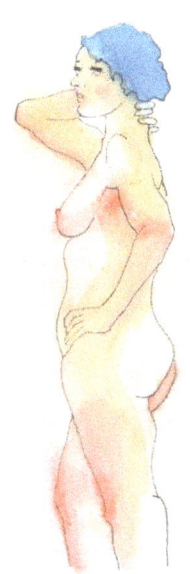

Using Black Markers & Watercolor Crayons (Inspired by Henri de Toulouse Lautrec)

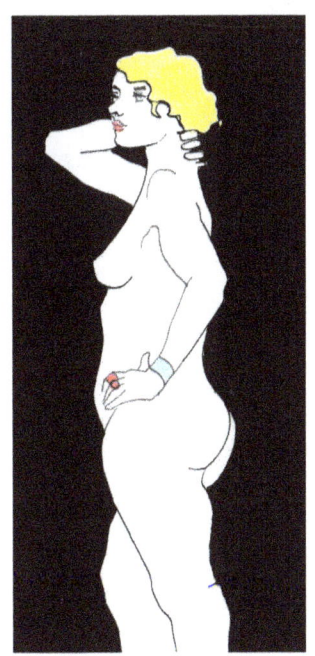

This drawing is inspired by the poster illustrations of Henri de Toulouse Lautrec. I kept it simple with just a few details highlighted in color and a black background.

Markers & Watercolors on Yupo Paper

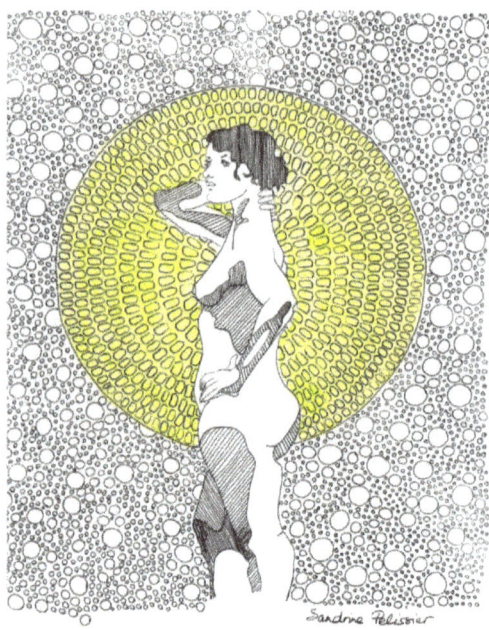

Using Marker & Watercolors (Inspired by Egon Schiele)

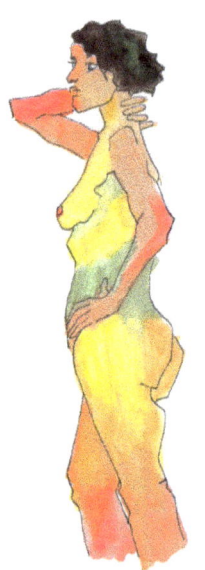

This piece is in the style of my "Life Patterns" series, where I re-work life drawings on Yupo paper with watercolor, markers, and many patterns.

When it comes to drawing, my favorite artist is Egon Schiele. This watercolor is inspired by some of his drawings. I did a black outline with marker, making the figure a bit more elongated and with sharp angles, then added color washes to the figure.

CHAPTER 9

Stamping Text onto Paintings or Drawings

Stamping is a fun, easy, and creative way to make unique drawings. You can start with an outline of the drawing you want to make and then stamp on some letters or shapes. The trick is to stamp more heavily where you want darker color and more lightly for lighter, less pigmented areas.

You will need

- Paper (I used cartridge paper)
- Stamps (smaller ones are easier to work with) or a pencil eraser
- A stamp pad
- A reference picture in black and white (so you can better see the contrast)

Stamping with Letters

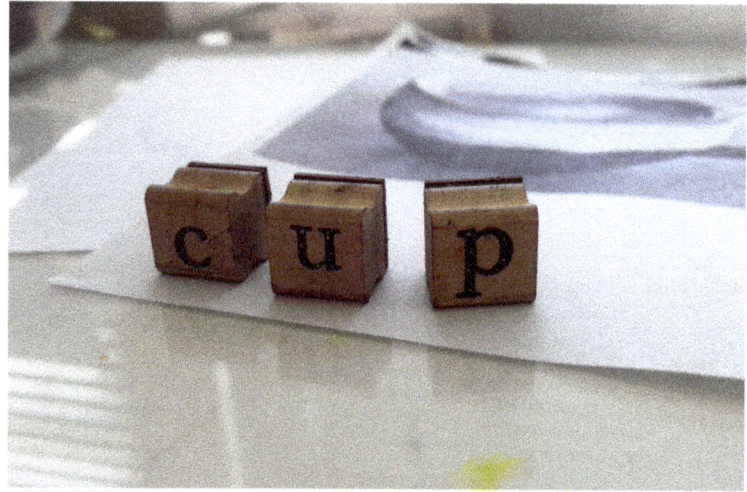

You can use letter stamps, stamps with designs, or even a pencil eraser.

Start by gathering some reference pictures of what you want to draw, and draw an outline of your object or figure. Choose the size of your stamp so that it is proportionate to the desired level of detail in your drawing.

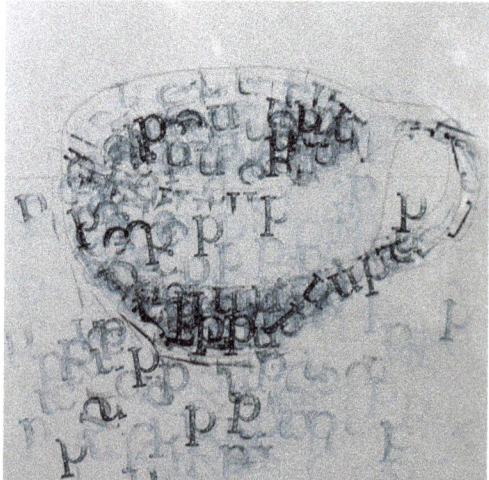

For this exercise, *I am stamping over a drawing of a coffee cup with the letters C, U and P. The drawing is large and not too detailed, so I can use larger letter stamps.*

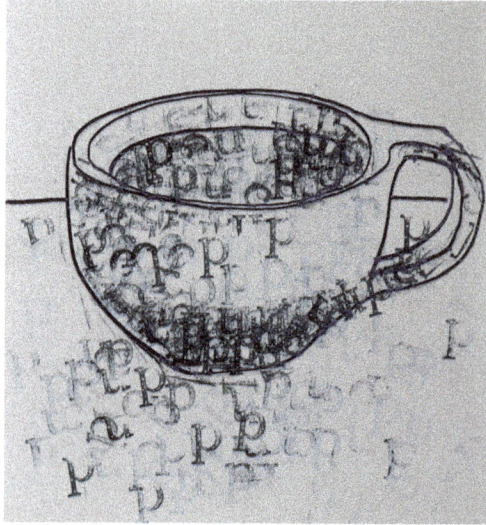

Use the stamp more times on the area you want to appear darker and less on the lighter areas. Above, I tried using only the stamp (left) and using the stamp with a thick outline to add definition.

TIP:
Try using white acrylic to clean up any stamping you want to remove.

Stamping with a Pencil Eraser

Because a pencil eraser is quite small, it will allow you to add more detail to a drawing.

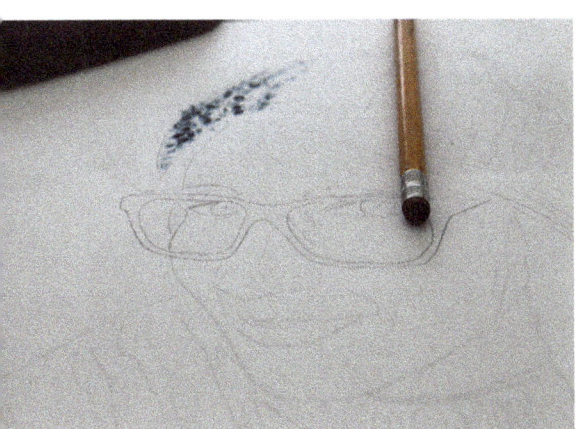

Use a stamp pad with your pencil eraser.

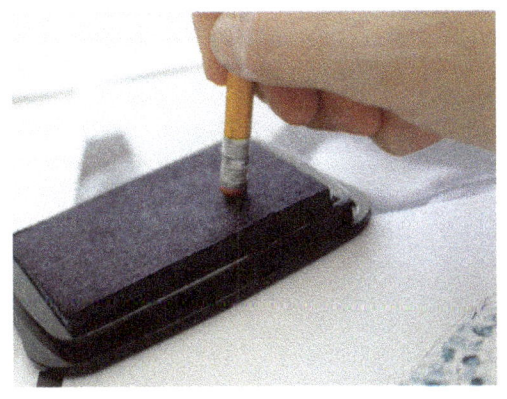

Again, stamp *more times on the area you wish to appear darker. Keep working on the drawing, one area at a time, all while looking at your reference picture.*

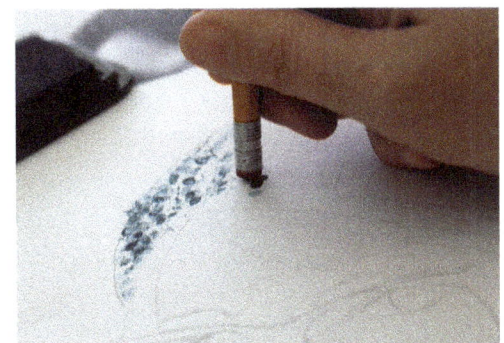

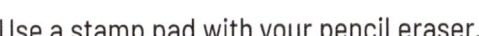

Here is my finished piece.

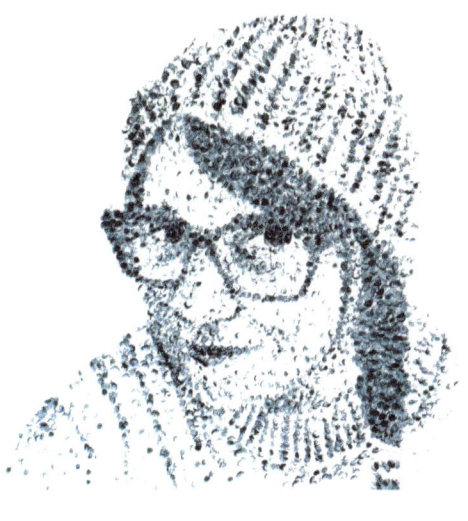

CHAPTER 10

The Beautiful Contrast of Lines and Washes

Sketching in pen and ink and adding watercolor washes after is a great way to give more life to your drawings. Watercolor and pen figure drawings have the perfect mix of precise sharp lines and loose washes of color.

This technique is also great for quick work: watercolor and ink dry quickly. Try taking your supplies outside for urban or landscape sketching.

For this exercise, you will need
- Some previously made life drawings
- A dipping pen
- Water-resistant black ink
- Watercolors
- A brush

printed a picture of my original drawing (left) and drew it onto a smaller watercolor paper (right).

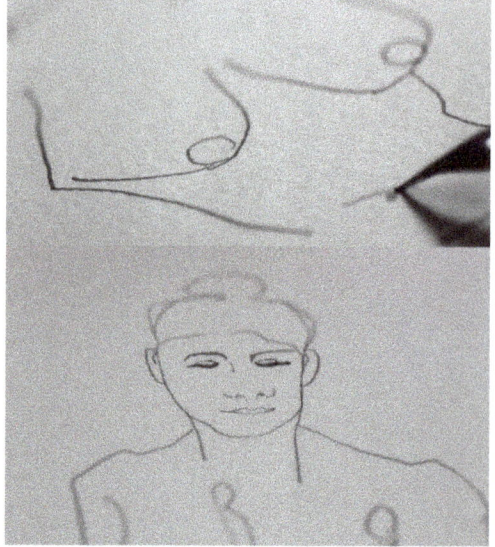

Begin by drawing free hand, rather than tracing your drawing, to keep the immediacy and fresh look of the original. Don't worry if your new drawing is not an exact reproduction or if the proportions are not perfect.

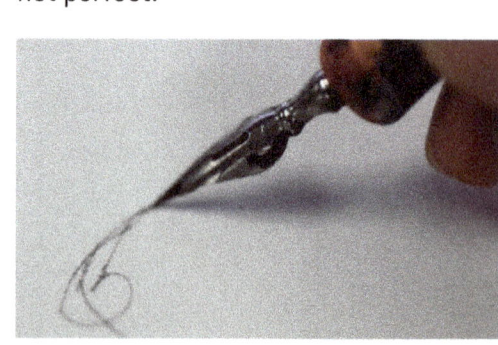

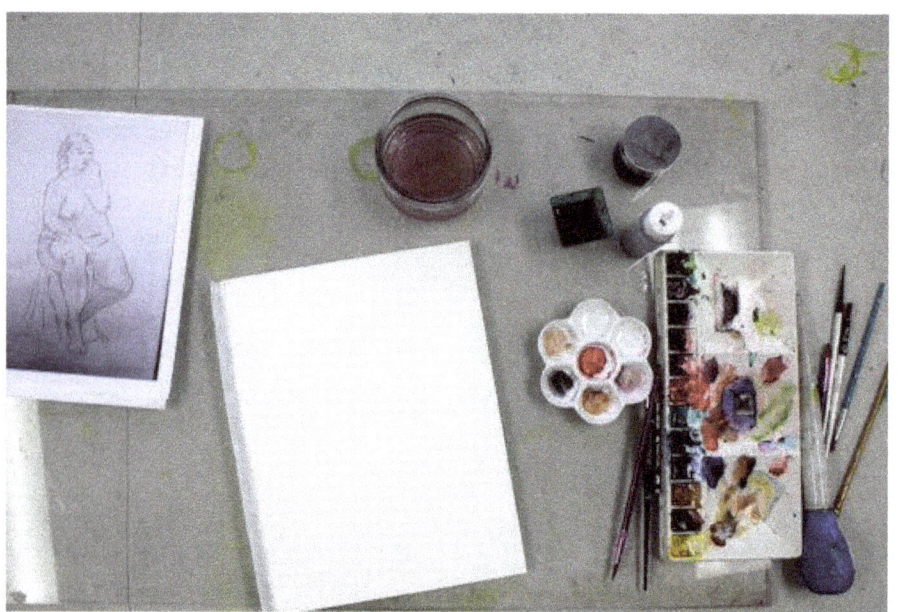

Start by making an outline of your drawing. Here, I am using the drawings I made in a life-drawing class. Because I worked on large, imperial-size paper in class, I

You can use a dipping pen for the drawing. I like dipping pens because they allow you to use any ink color you mix, they are affordable, and they never dry out.

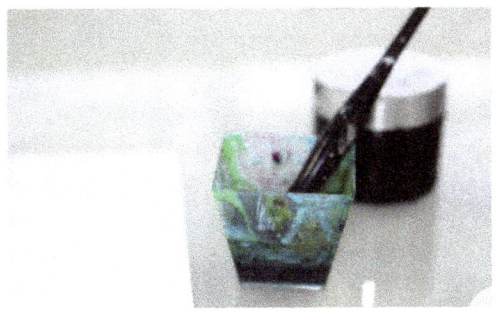

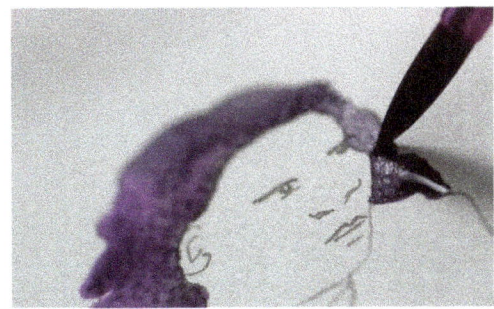

 TIP:
To get a medium gray that is a bit softer than black, mix a bit of India ink with water.

When you begin painting, there are a few methods you can try. You can paint the light color washes and then the darker colors, or you can paint from the top of the figure to the bottom and let the colors mix, wet into wet. Here, I used the second technique, starting with a dark purple wash for the hair.

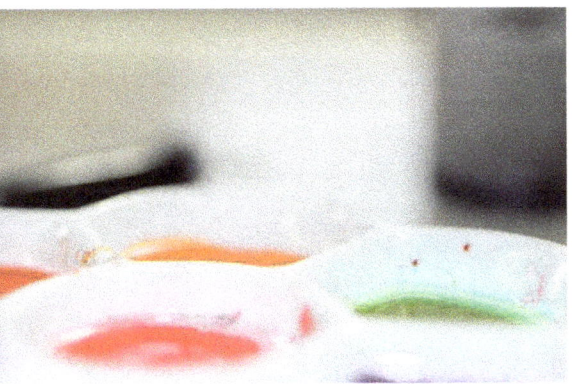

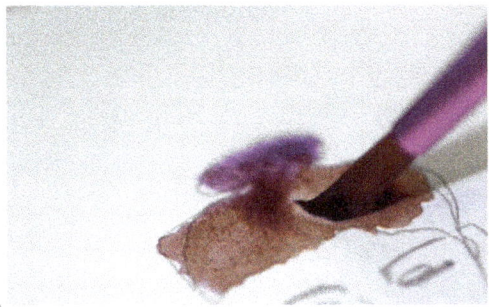

Next, mix a few watercolor washes. The colors you use don't need to be realistic; the colors themselves matter more than their tonal values.

You can also try mixing two different colors for one area (wet-into-wet technique).

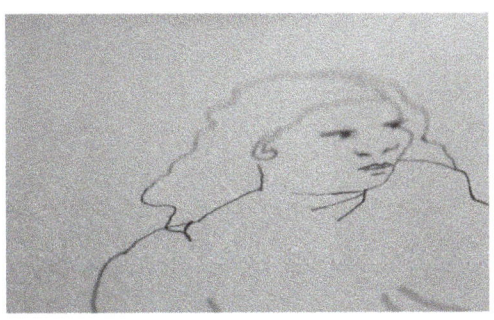

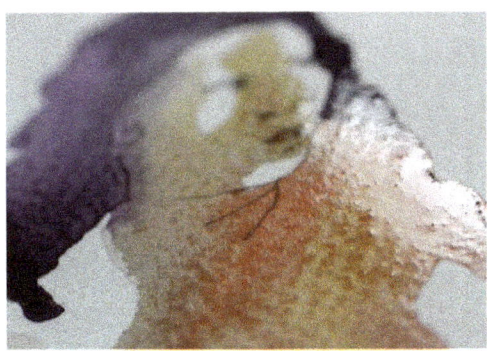

Continue painting washes of watercolor wet into wet, letting the colors bleed into each other and keeping some areas of highlights unpainted.

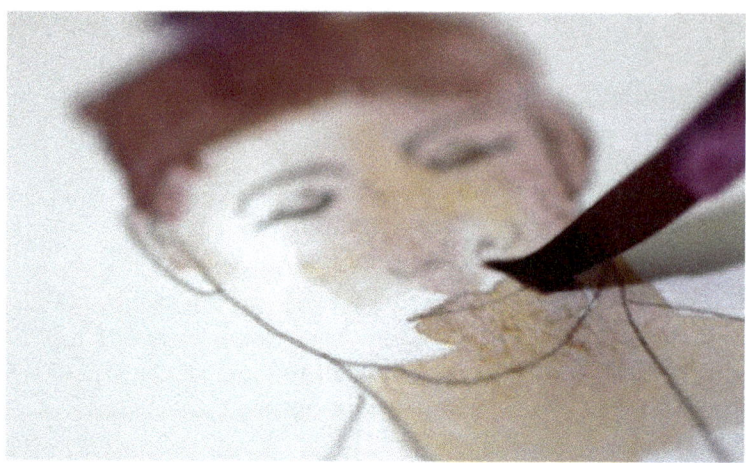

You can also soften some edges by painting over them with a brush using just water.

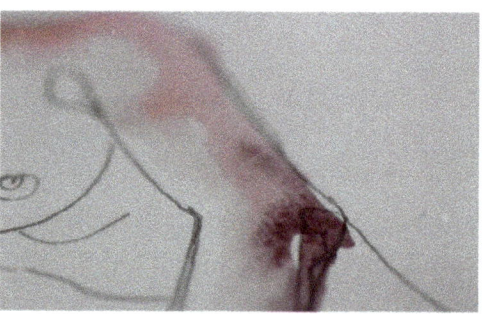

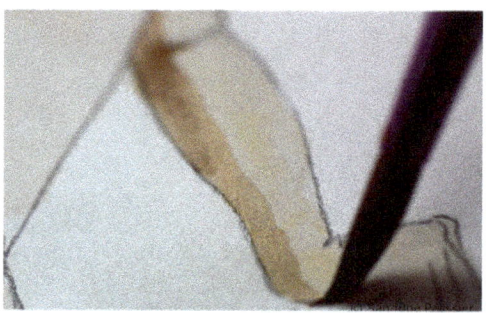

Continue painting the whole figure.

Another technique you can try is painting the lighter washes first and letting them dry before painting another darker layer in a few areas.

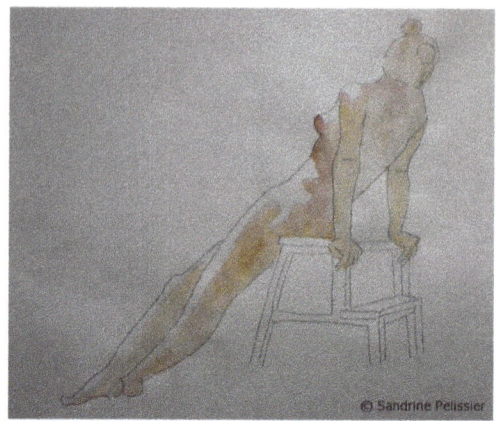

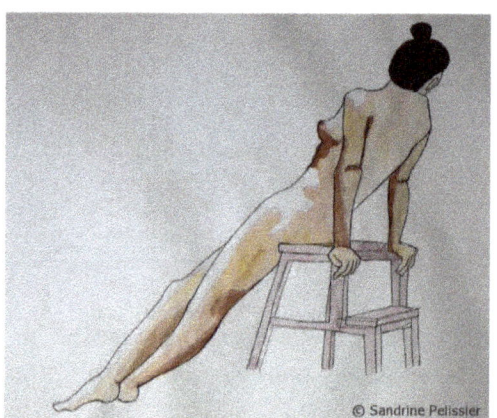

Here are some examples of watercolor and pen figure drawings:

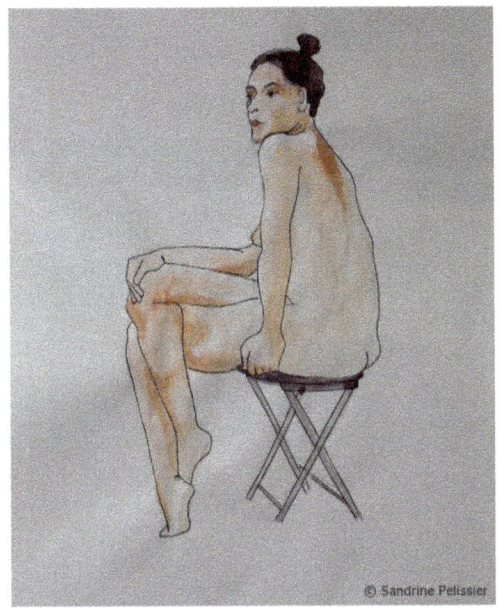

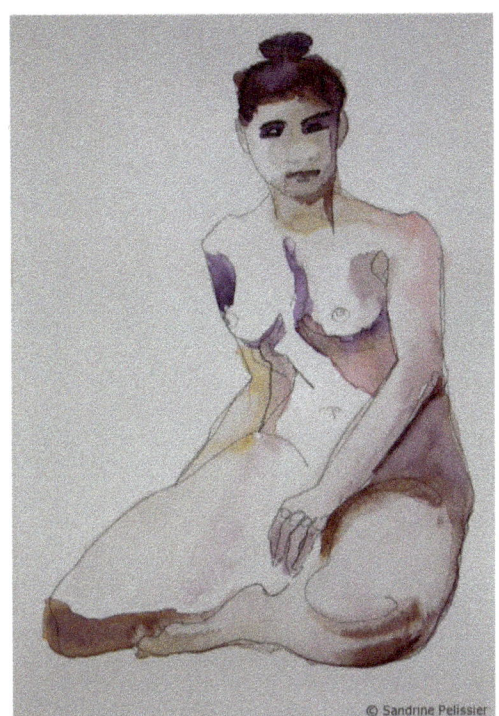

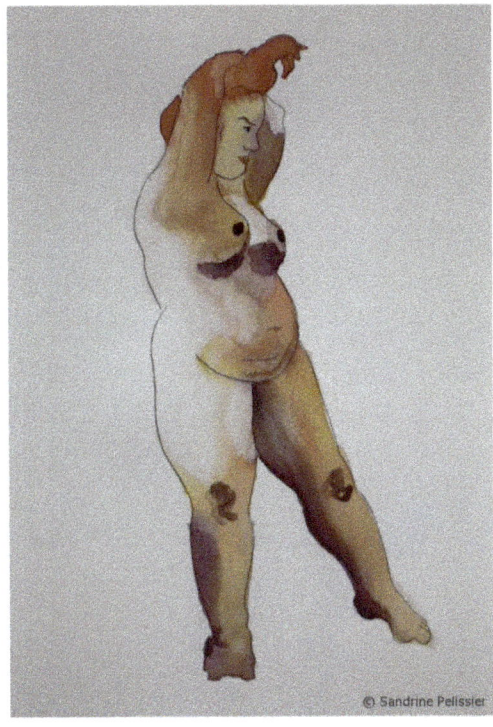

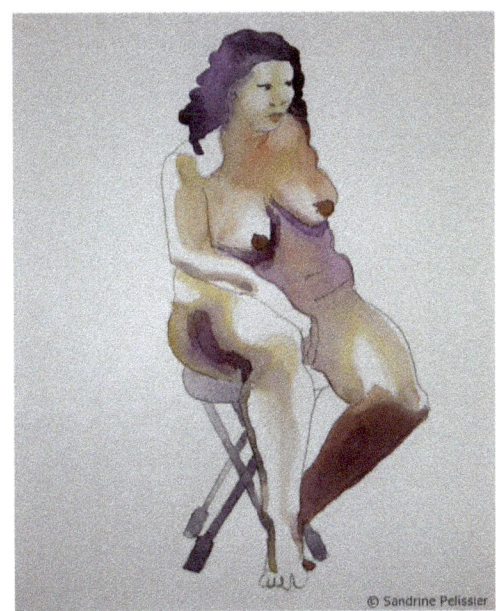

CHAPTER 11

Figure Drawing

Life drawing can grow frustrating: practicing can become repetitive and it takes a lot of time to improve. Here are five ideas to help bring the fun back to life drawing!

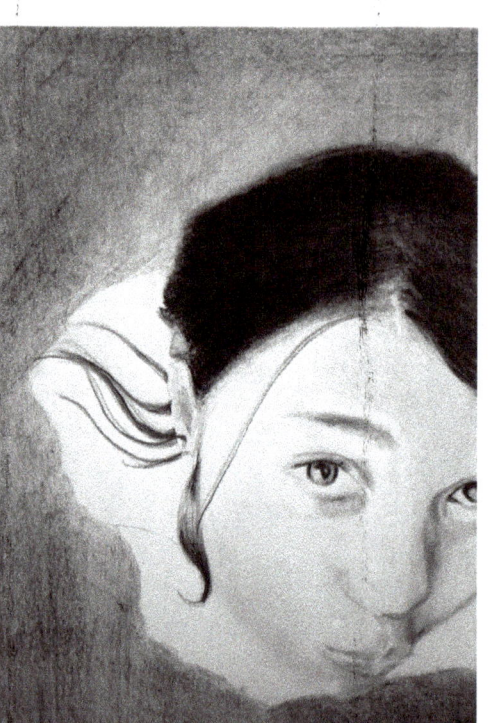

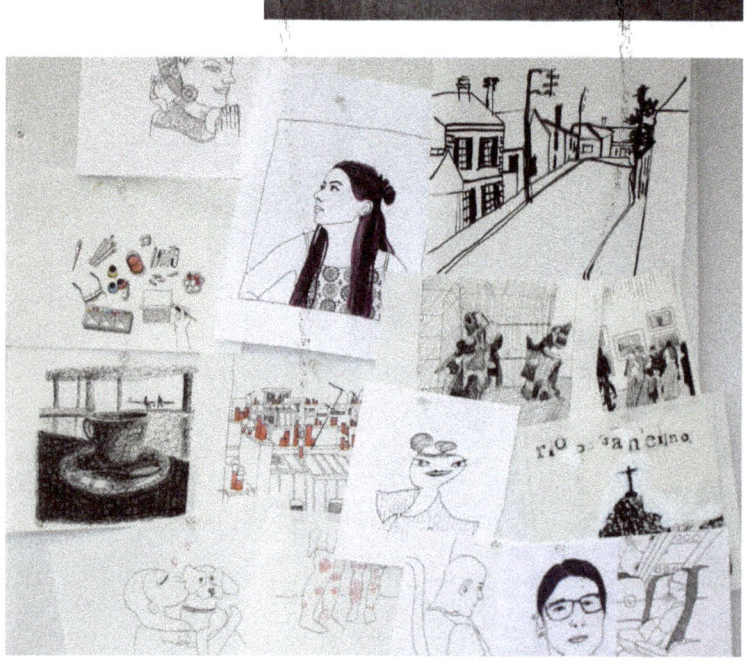

It is interesting to try many different drawing techniques so you never get stuck in one particular style and can explore different avenues. There is a world of possibilities beyond classical drawing.

Using Several Pencils At Once

Simply hold a few colored pencils in your hand at the same time and begin to draw. Depending on the way you move your hand and the pressure you apply to each, you will create unique overlapping lines and textures.

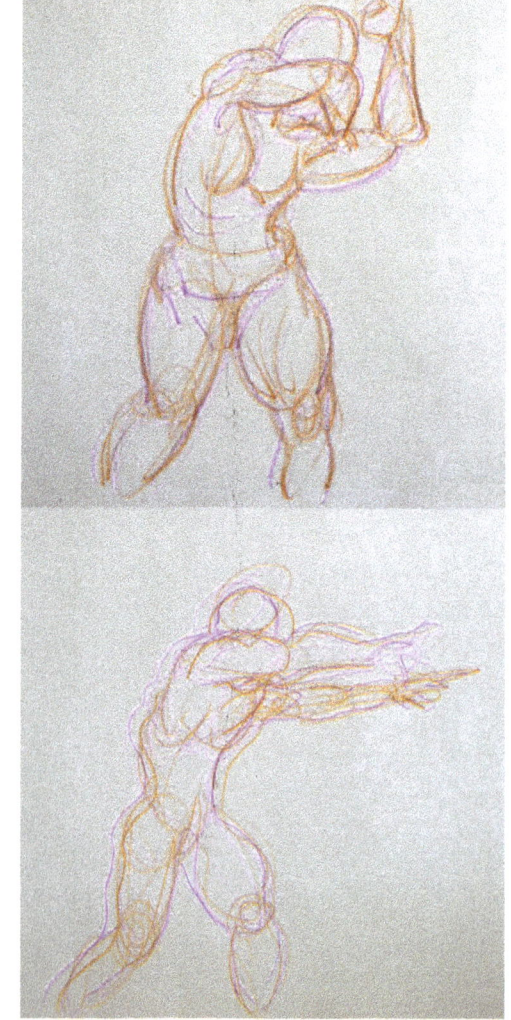

Drawing Without Lifting Your Pencil

This exercise is all about rhythm: try to keep the pencil on the paper and moving for the entire time you draw.

One way to simplify this technique is to think about where the volumes of your figure or object are and illustrate them using rounded motions, as in the examples below.

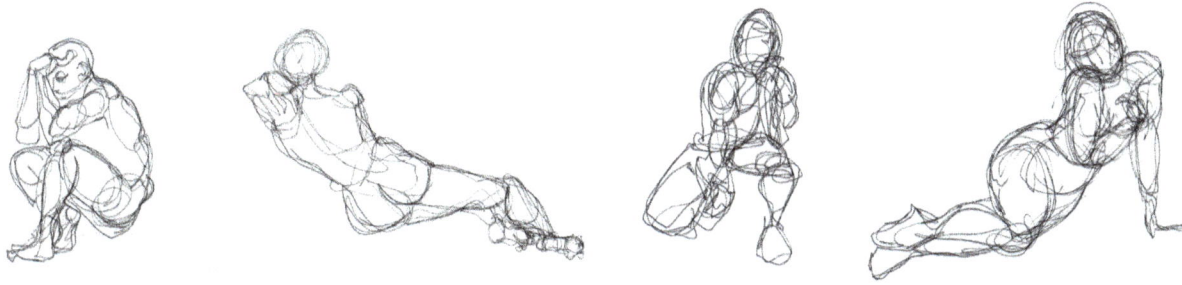

Drawing With a Stick

It may be hard to believe, but sometimes you can get great results by making life drawing more difficult than it already is! Drawing with a natural wooden stick dipped in ink is difficult, but the drawings you create with it have an interesting raw energy.

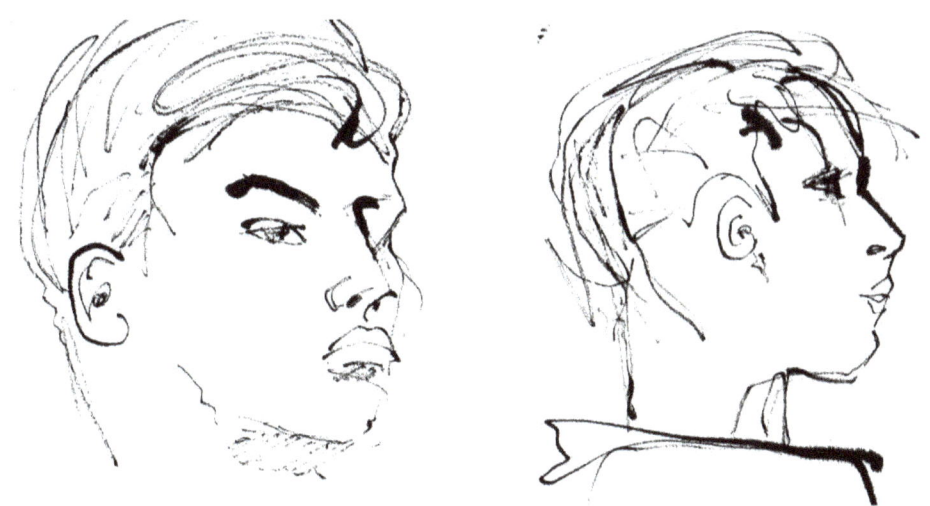

 TIP:
You can use the same technique of drawing with a stick for any type of art: figures, landscapes, still life, etc.

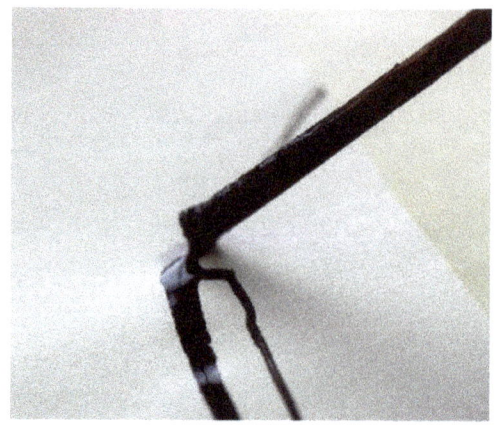
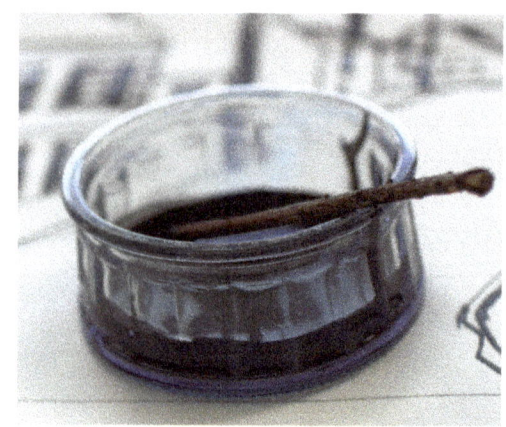

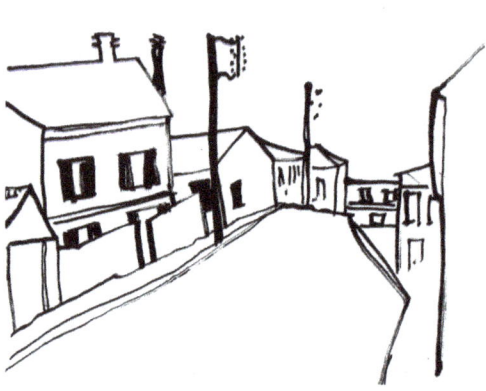
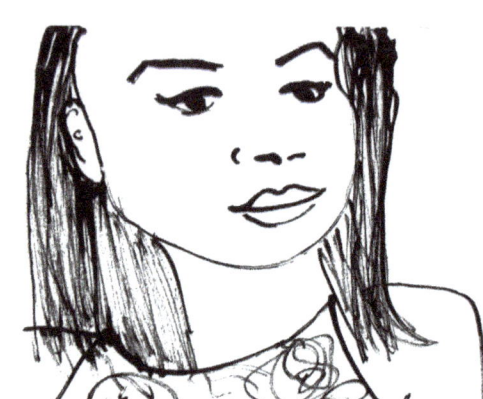

Beauty is Confidence, Not Perfection

Drawing weekly for a few years now, my perception of what constitutes a good drawing has evolved over the years.

Nowadays, I don't worry about being perfectly accurate in my proportions or being realistic or even achieving a perfect likeness of a model. I am more satisfied by the idea of making a drawing I like—in all its imperfections.

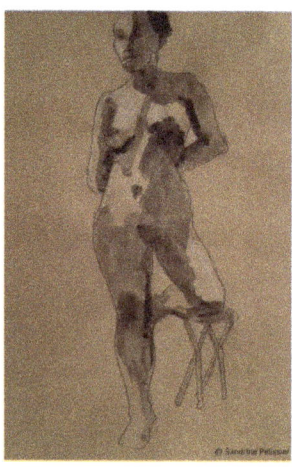
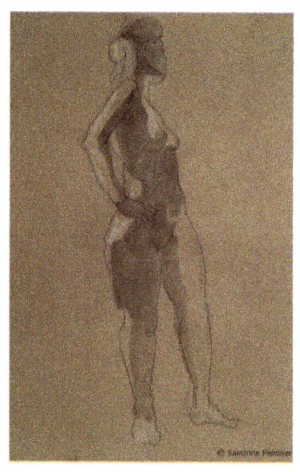
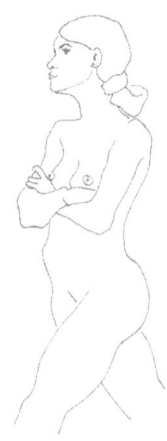
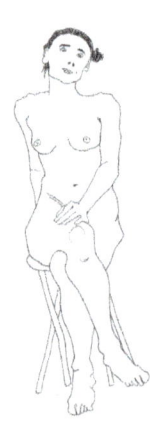

Some of my favorite drawings of all time are some of the ones that look the strangest!

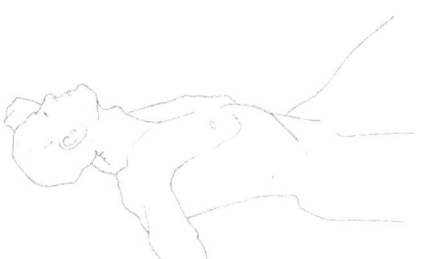

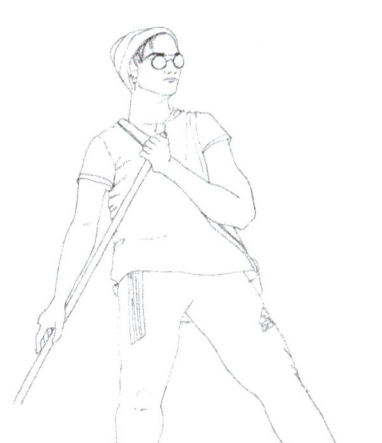

One of the best pieces of advice I've read about life drawing is to use ink (a marker or dipping pen) instead of a pencil. Most of us have a tendency to fuss over the lines we just made. Drawing with ink removes that temptation: all lines become definitive and errors must be integrated. This is a great way to gain confidence while you make art.

Variety Is the Spice of Life (Drawing)

Attending a weekly class, doing the same exercises over and over again, can be-

come quite repetitive. A way to break this monotony is to experiment with different papers and media.

Try using white paper, medium-toned paper (on which you can add white highlights), and black paper.

For drawing tools, try using markers, watercolor, charcoal, graphite, felt tip pens, watercolor crayons, and pastels.

Here are a few ideas to experiment with:

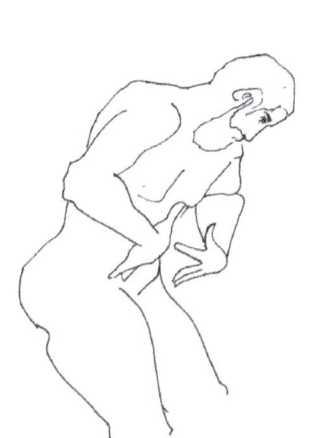

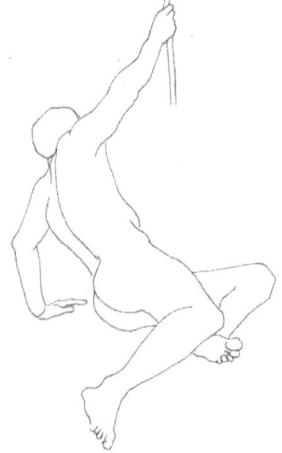

Try different styles, like a simple ink outline drawing.

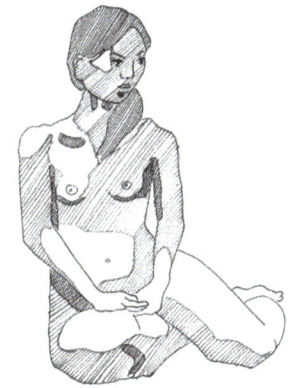

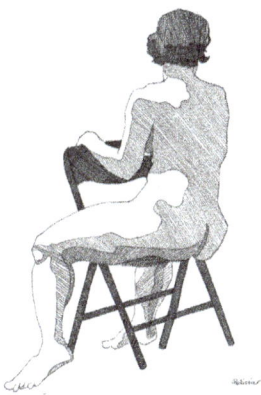

Try adding shading to your ink drawings with hatching.

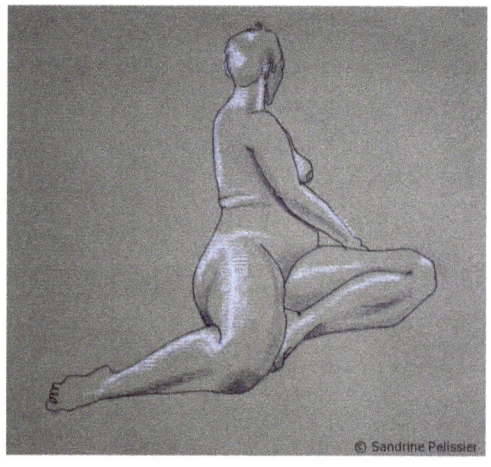

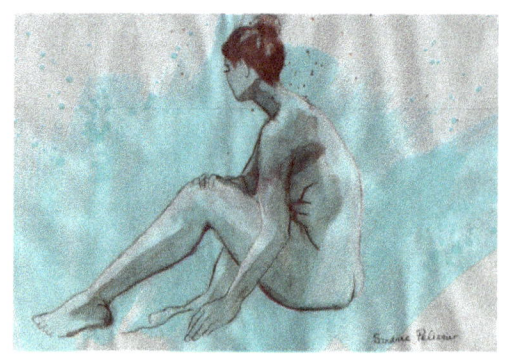

Try drawing on top of a few strokes of paint. You can paint a few paper sheets before going to class so they are dry and ready to be used.

Try drawing on medium-toned paper and adding white highlights.

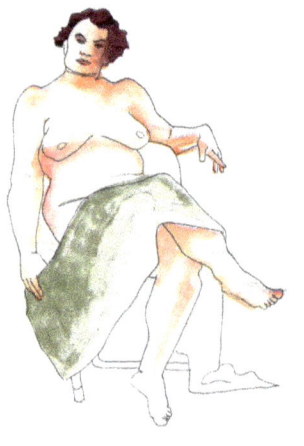

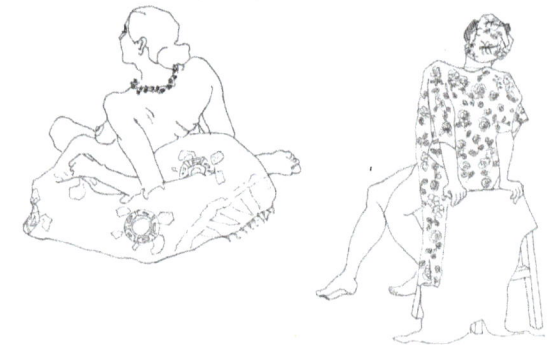

Try focusing on patterns like fabrics and jewelry in your drawings.

Try adding splashes of color with water-colors.

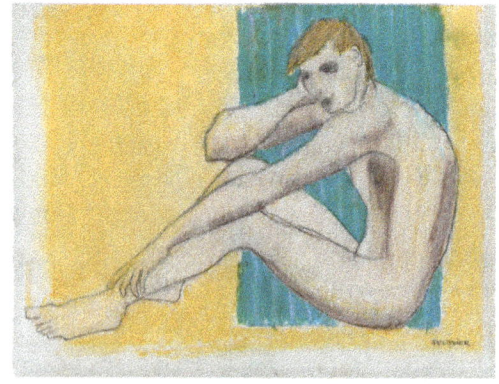

Try reworking your old drawings; you can use dry pastels or washes of color and add patterns.

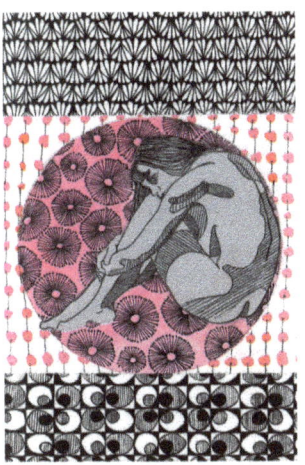 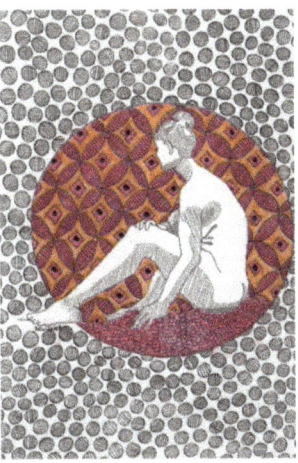 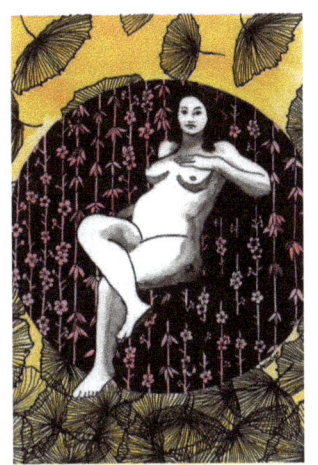 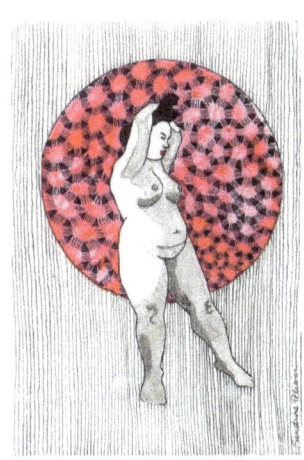

Examples of drawings reworked with watercolor washes and patterns in ink.

You can also try "dressing" your models by adding patterned clothes on top of a nude drawing as I did in the examples below:

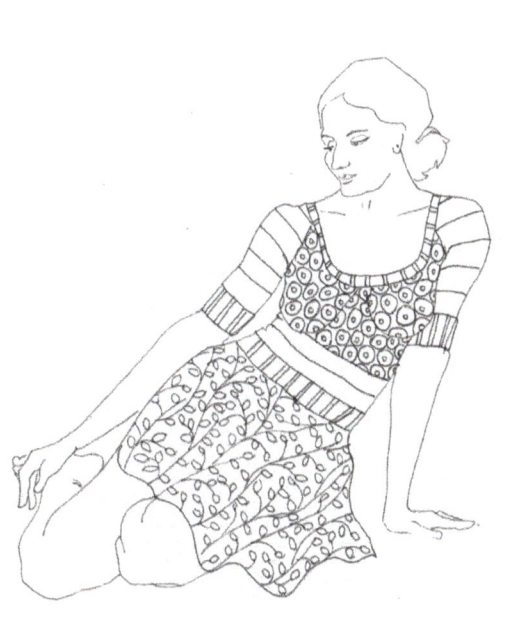

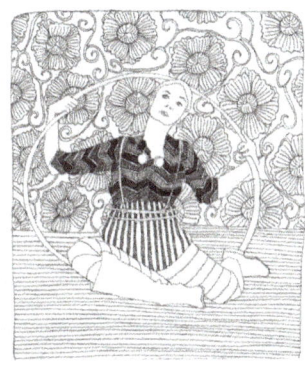

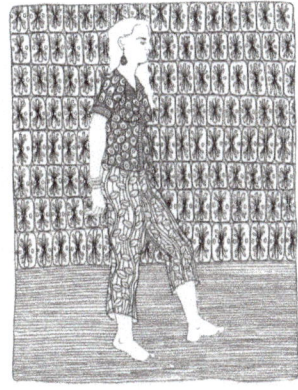

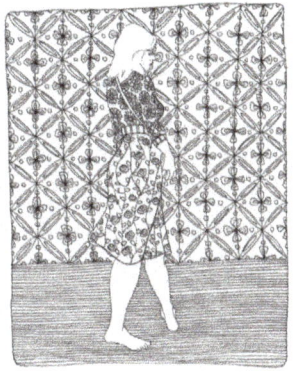

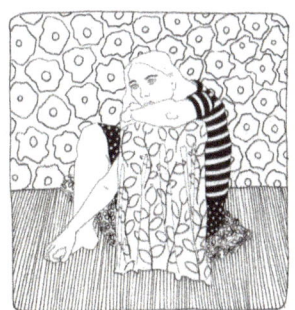

CHAPTER 12

Between Drawing and Painting

The definition of what constitutes a drawing is not always simple. Sometimes a drawing is defined by the tools used (pen, pencil, crayon). Sometimes it is defined by the use of lines. Sometimes the absence of color is a factor.

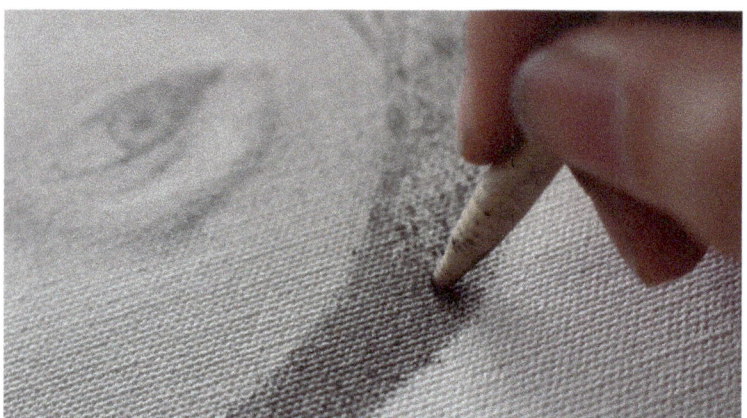

Example of smudging pencil on canvas

The truth is that many artworks fall somewhere in between drawings and paintings. This is true for anything done with pastels, India ink, or pencil works on canvas. To make things more confusing, you can even apply a drawing medium like charcoal with a brush or make a drawing with a painting medium, such as dry brushing with oil paint.

It can be fun to explore the area between drawing and painting—or even mix elements of drawing and painting, line and wash. Here are a few techniques you can explore that fall somewhere between drawing and painting.

Adding Patterns to Your Painting

Try using a drawing tool like a dipping pen to add patterns to elements of your painting. Here, I covered a forest painting in black and white patterns using a dipping pen and India ink:

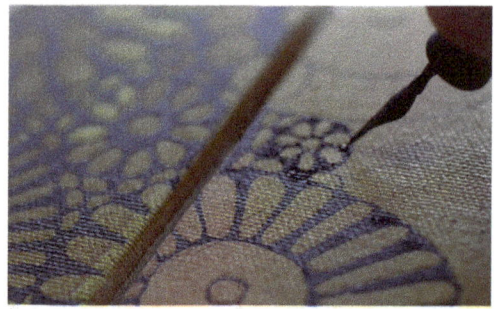

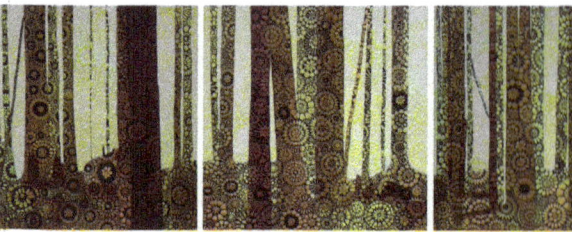

"Forest Lace" (Acrylic on canvas)

In the following example, I used a dipping pen to add repetitive patterns around figures drawn on canvas:

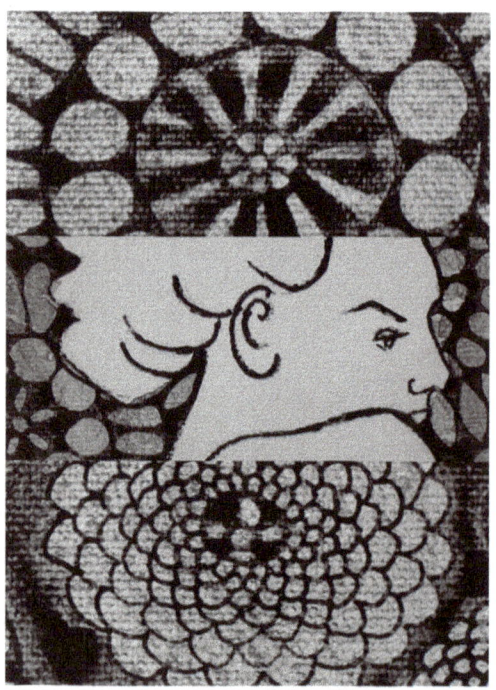

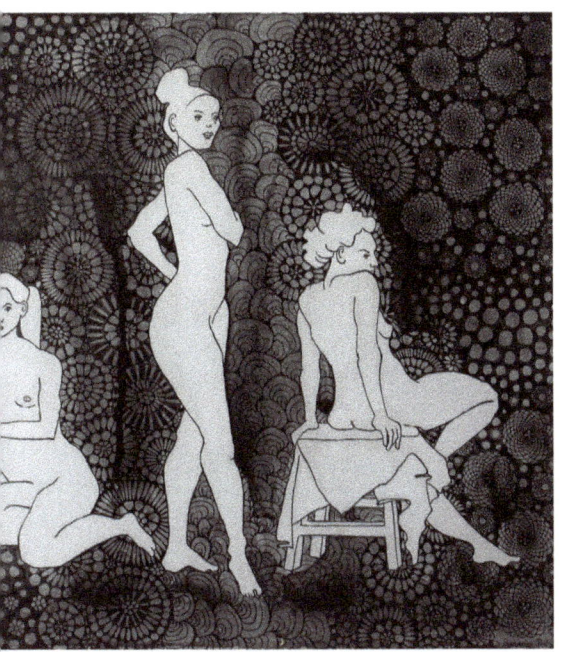

"Social Fabric II," details and full painting (Acrylic on Canvas)

Drawing Lines On Canvas

You can also try creating a picture using only lines on canvas. These can be loops, straight lines, patterns, or scribbles.

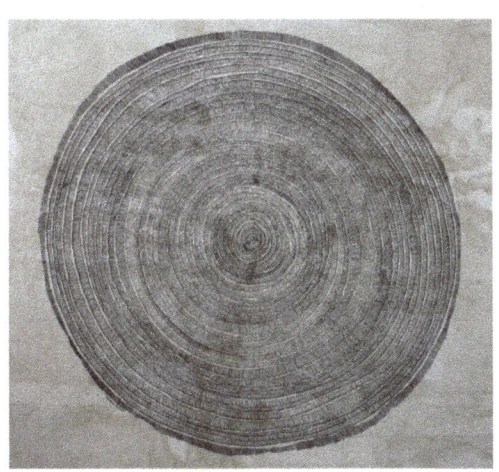

Example of a painting done entirely with a fountain pen, India ink, and lots and lots of loops!

Example of loops drawn with a dipping pen on canvas to make a tree cookie design.

Here is another example of a painting made only with lines. In this case, the lines represent the negative space of the image.

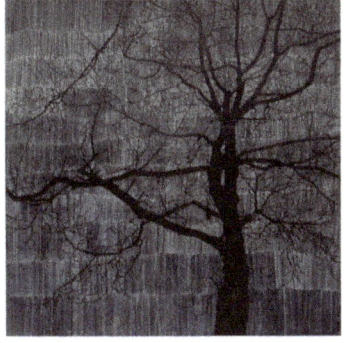

"Timelines 2" (Fluid Acrylic on Canvas). All lines are straight and done with a dipping pen.

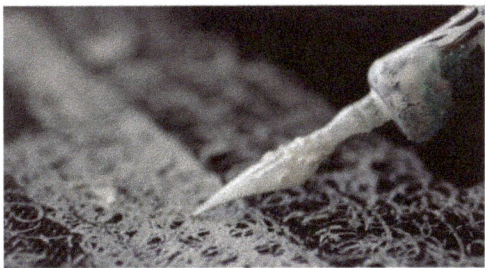

You can also use scribblings to make an image.

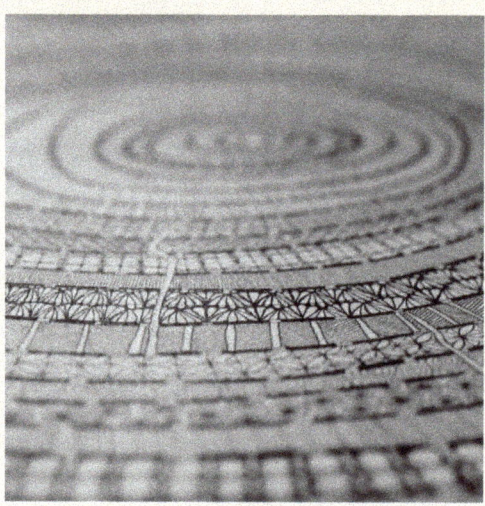

"Raveled," painting done with white scribblings of fluid acrylic on canvas.

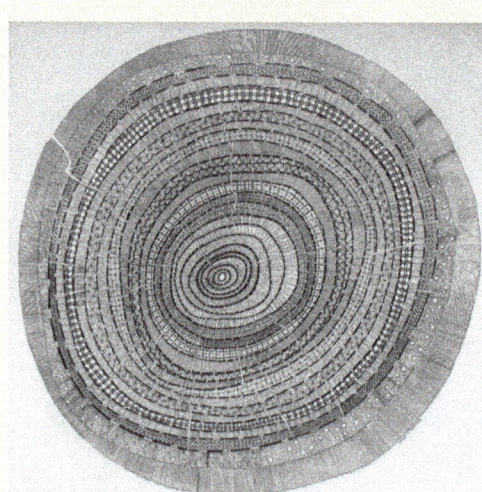

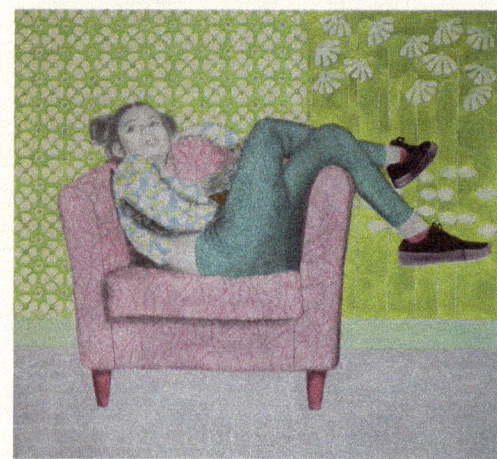

A cookie tree painting made on canvas, done entirely with patterns.

Drawing with Pencil, Charcoal, or Dry Brush on Canvas

You can use pencils on canvas, but be sure to fix the graphite with fixative before varnishing.

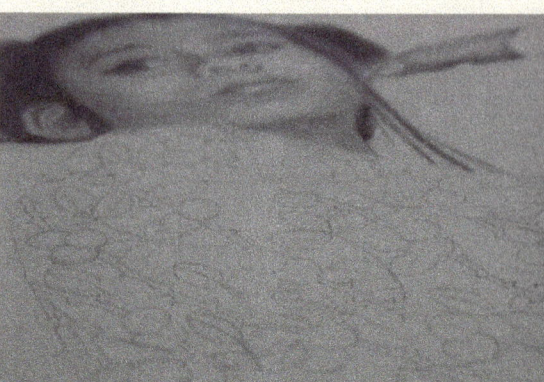

"Slice of Life II- Louise" (Graphite and Fluid Acrylic on Canvas)

Only parts of this painting of my daughter Louise are done with pencil. The rest of the patterns are drawn and painted with fluid acrylic.

In this portrait on my daughter Charlotte, I worked on paper that was mounted on a board. Parts of the portrait were drawn with charcoal, while the rest was painted with fluid acrylics. Most of the charcoal was applied and blended with a brush. I used larger brushes for large areas and smaller brushes for the details.

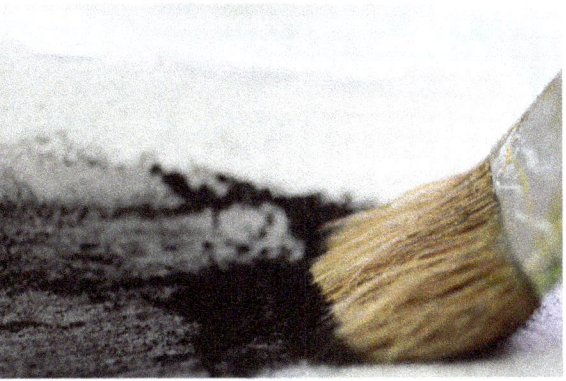

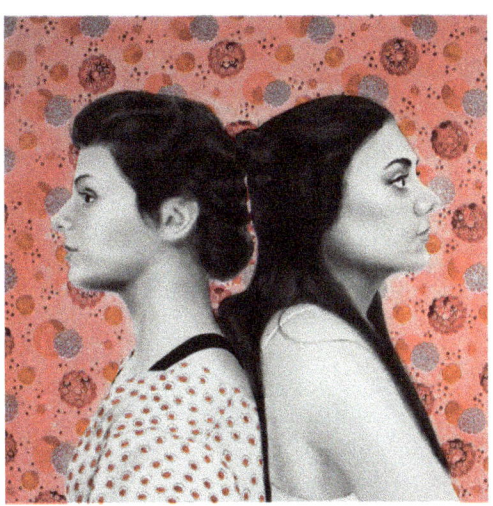

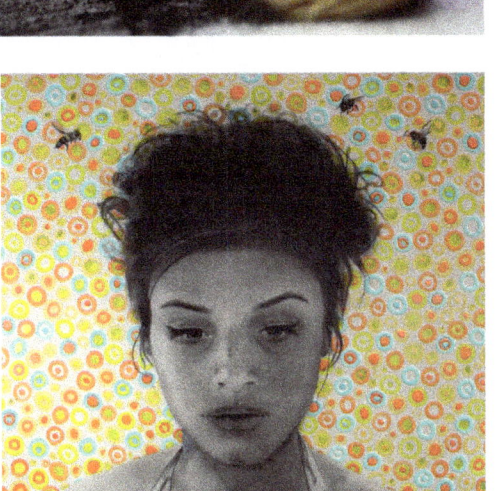

"Slice of Life, Beehive" (Charcoal, Acrylic, and Pastel on Board-Mounted Paper).

Dry brushing is another fun technique in which you draw with a brush lightly dipped in oil paint.

For this exercise, begin by spreading a bit of paint on a piece of canvas that you will use as a palette.

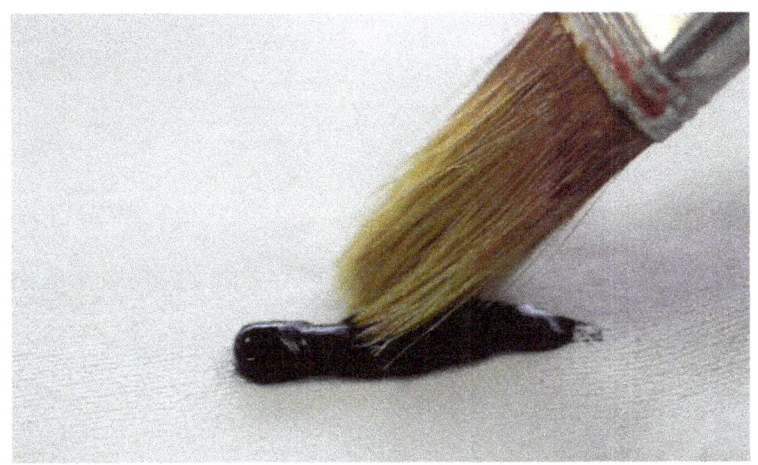

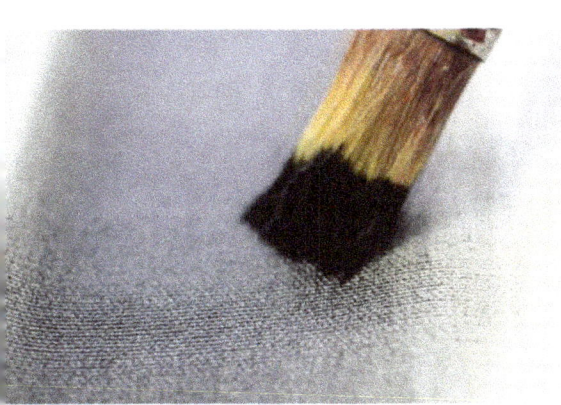

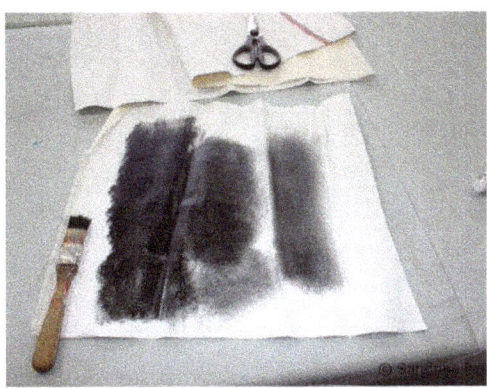

My palette (after use).

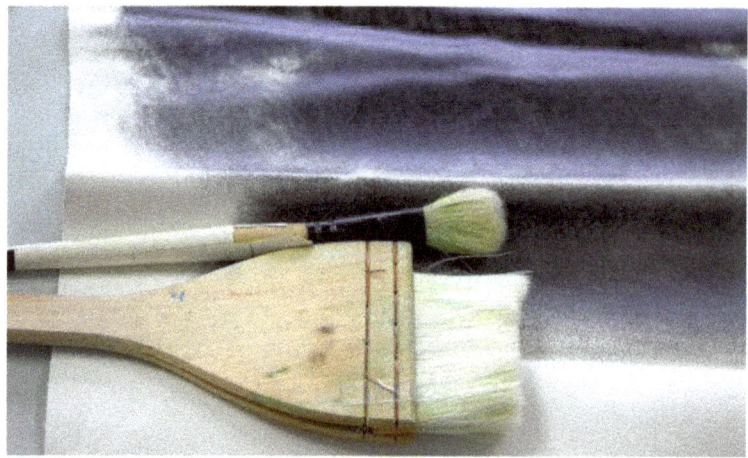

You can use soft brushes for lighter areas where you want softer edges and smaller, stiff brushes for darker details to create hard edges.

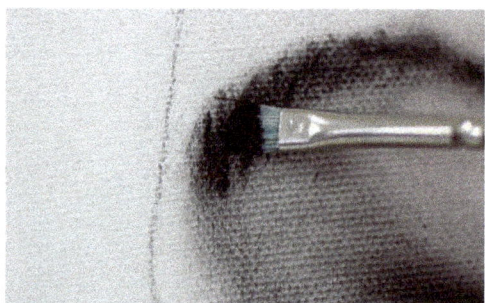

Example of using a small stiff brush on details.

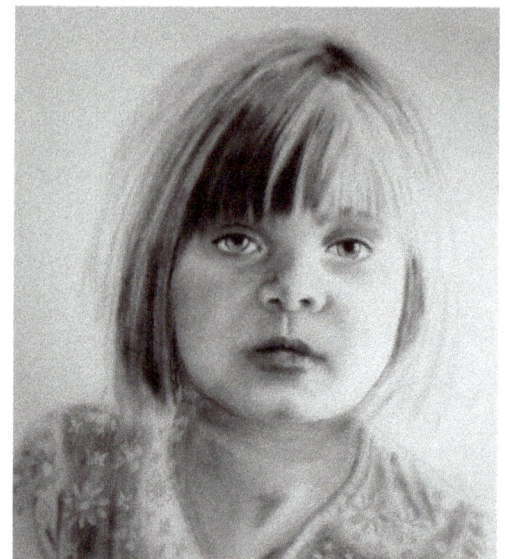

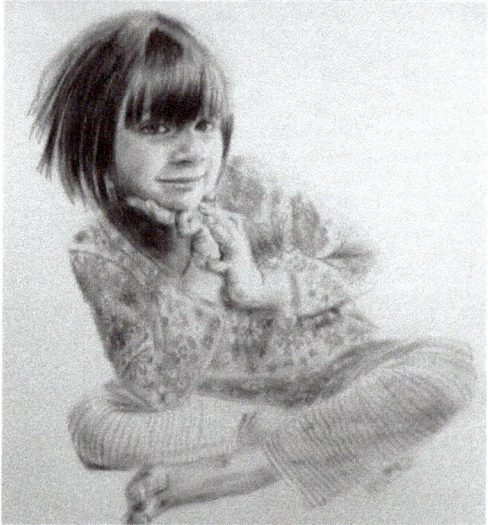

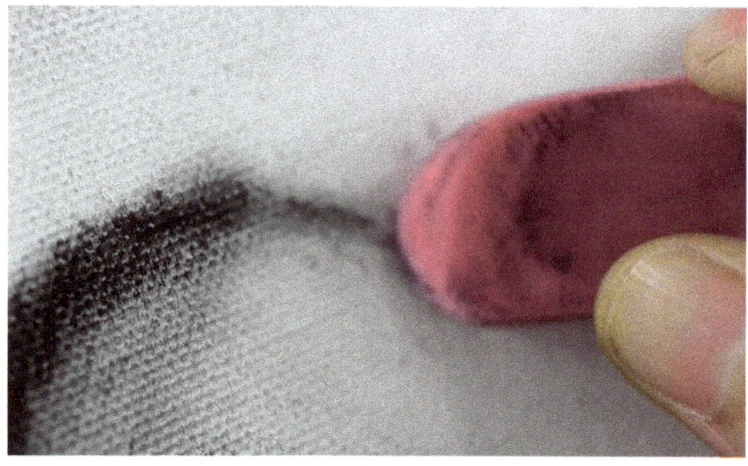

You can even erase some of the paint with a regular eraser.

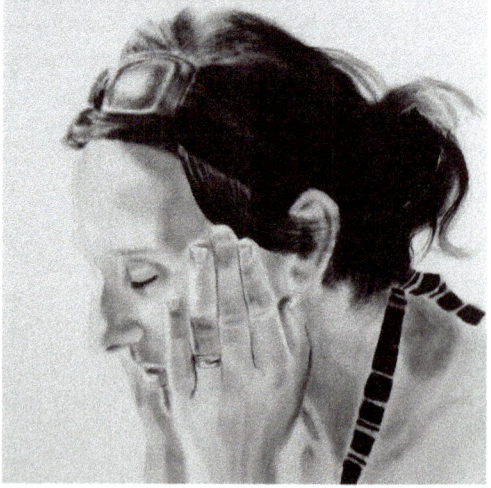

Examples of dry brushing on canvas and paper.

Using a Drawing Medium as Paint

Some drawing media can actually be used as paint when mixed with water, such as charcoal or dry pastels.

You can also use PanPastels as paint by mixing them with water in their pans or other rounded containers

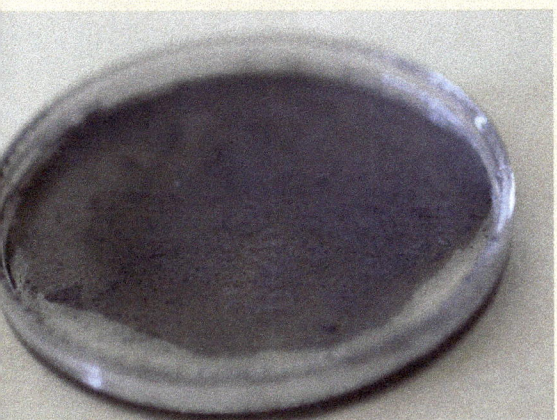

Here, I used Kraft paper and a water-brush.

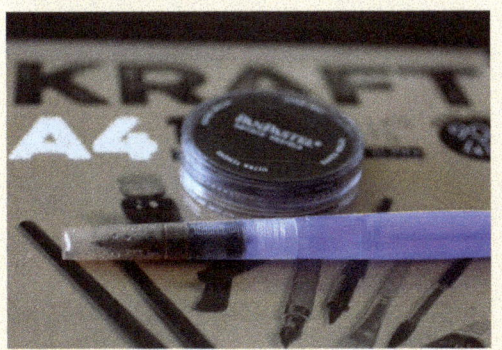

You can even erase areas when they have had time to dry.

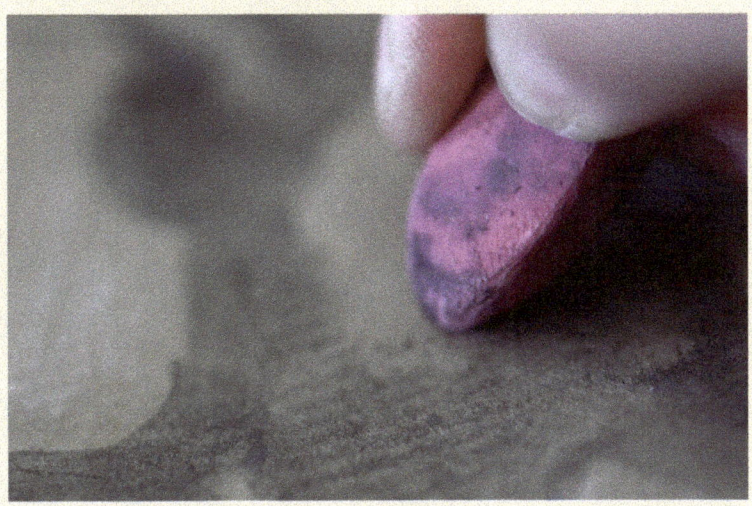

The pastel will create lovely textures when mixed with water.

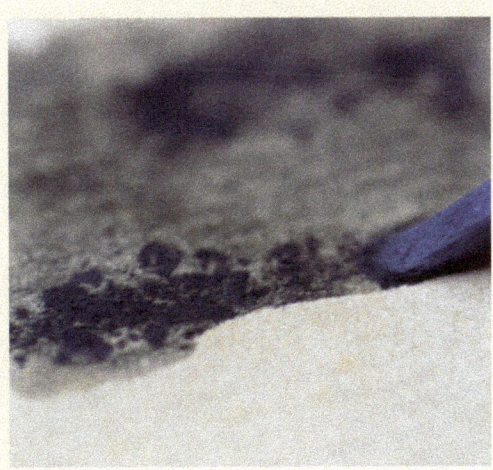

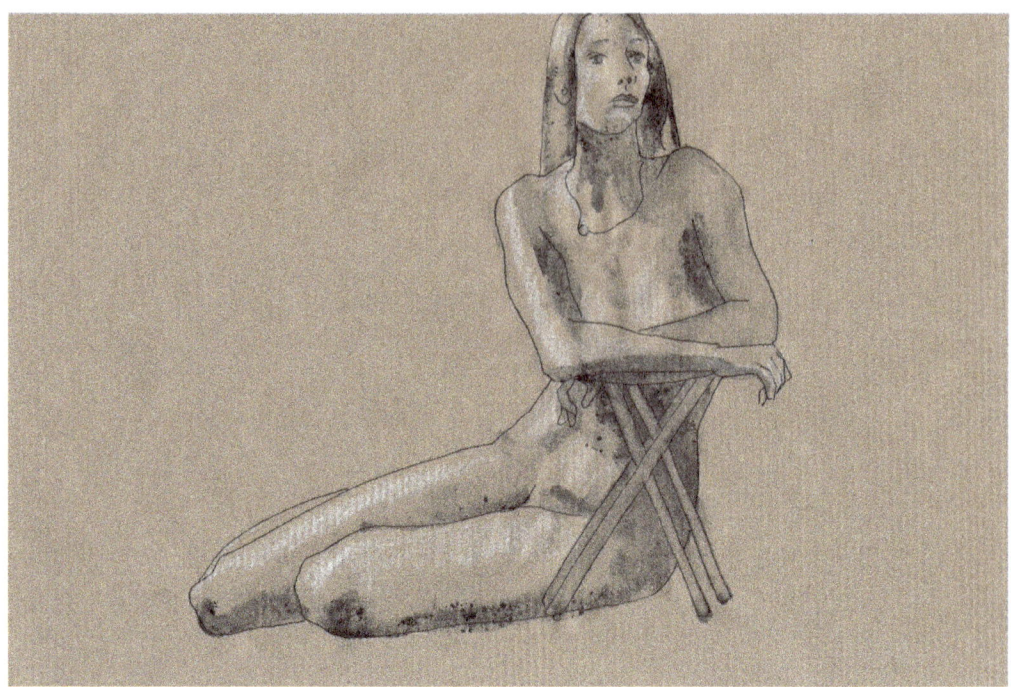

*Example of a painting on Kraft paper made using
PanPastels mixed with water.*

CHAPTER 13

Simple Monoprint Techniques

The No-Phone Selfie

The "no-phone" selfie is a simple technique to draw a self portrait directly on a mirror and make a monoprint that you can later rework.

For this exercise, you will need
- A small mirror
- Cartridge paper
- Washable felt pens
- A spray bottle filled with water
- Glass cleaner

Start by cleaning your mirror with glass cleaner.

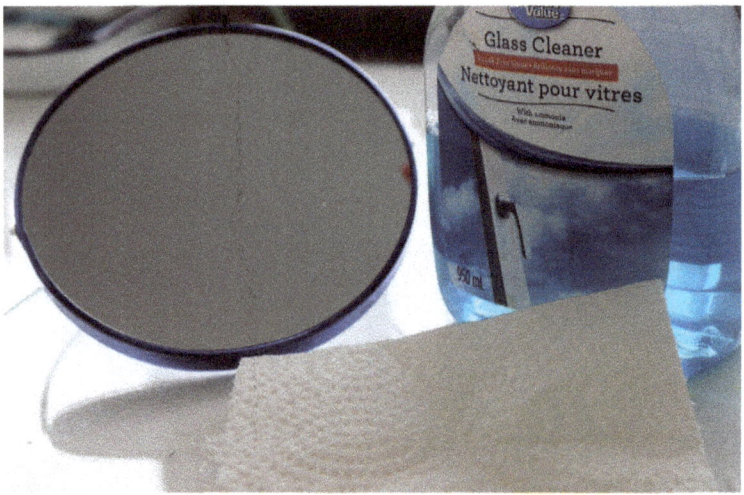

Then, select a few colors of washable pens you would like to use.

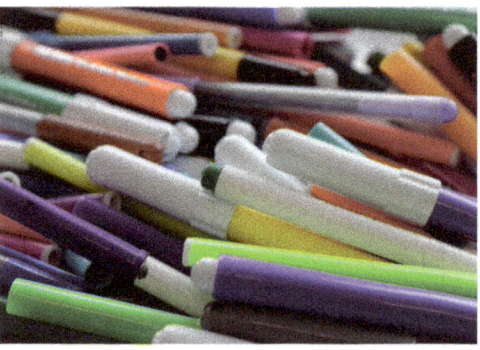

Next, draw the outlines of your face and your features directly on the mirror with washable felts. You might need to close one eye, then the other, to better see what you are drawing on the mirror. When you switch eyes, align the outlines of your drawing with your reflection before you continue.

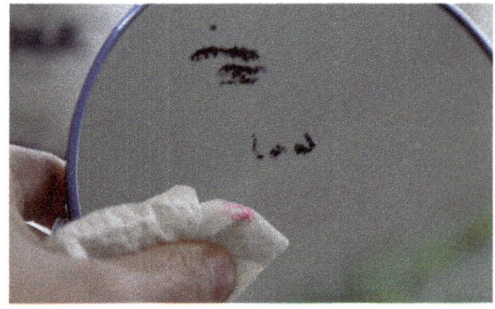

Continue drawing until you are satisfied with your portrait, using various colors if desired.

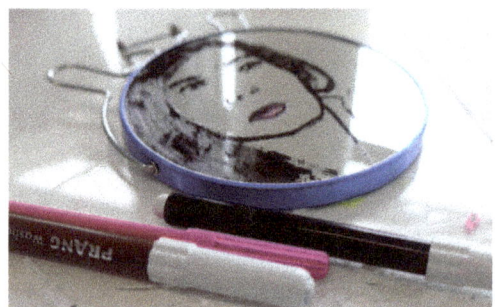

You can adjust your drawing once you are done tracing the contours of your face.

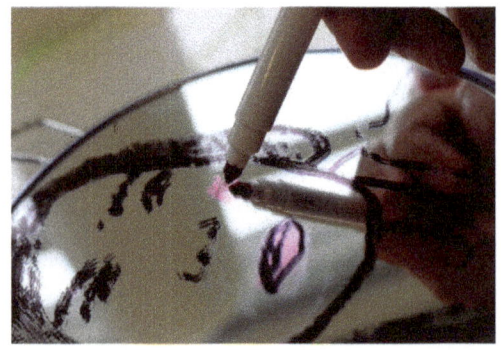

Here, I added a background, as well.

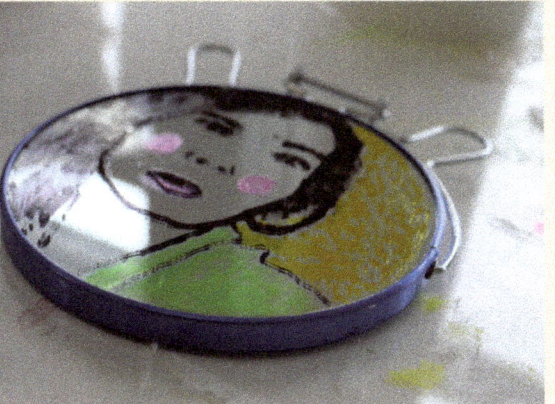

Next, spray a piece of paper that is the same size as your mirror (printer paper will work) with water. You can experiment with different degrees of dampness for various effects. I find it works best when you spray the paper and then remove excess water with a tissue.

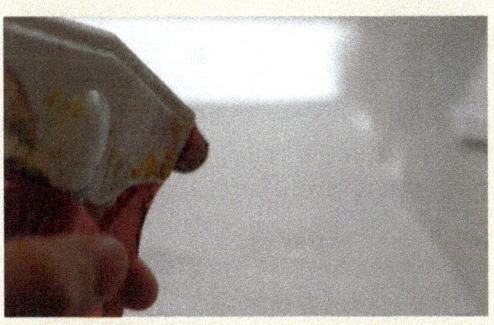

Place your damp paper onto the mirror and press down with your hand, slowly and firmly.

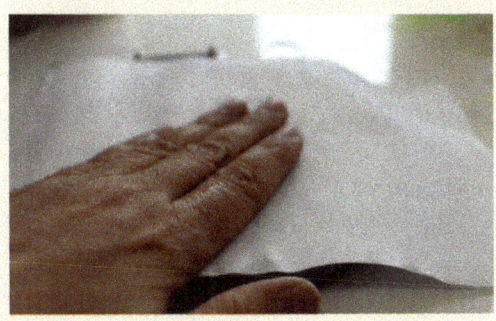

After a few seconds, lift the paper to reveal your drawing, which has transferred onto it.

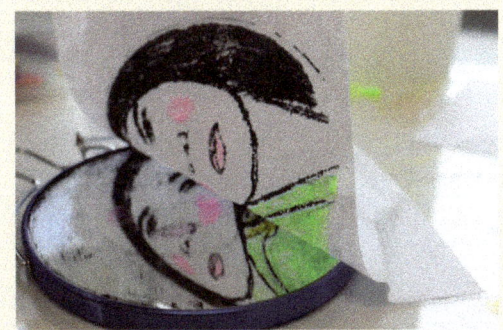

Here is my finished drawing.

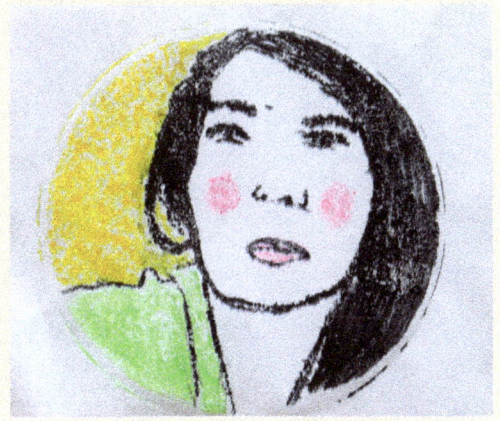

Sometimes, you may have enough left on the mirror to make another print or two.

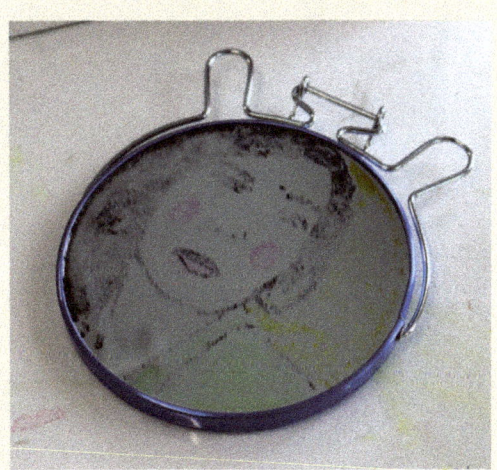

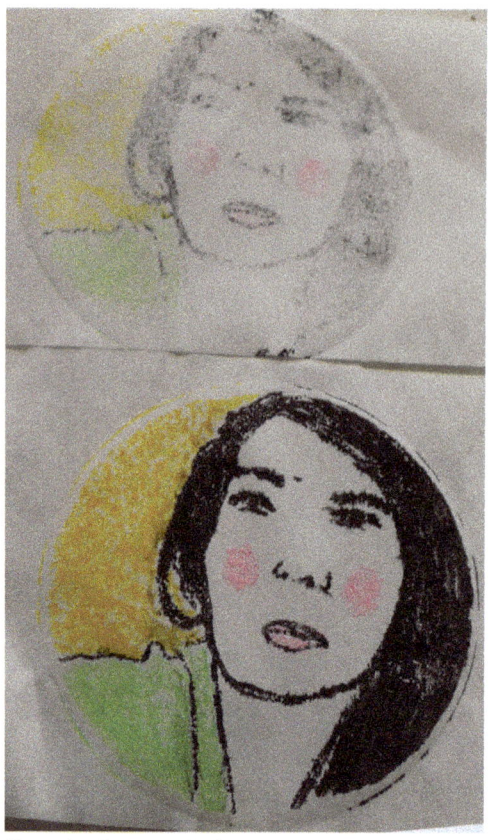

Example of a second print and an initial print.

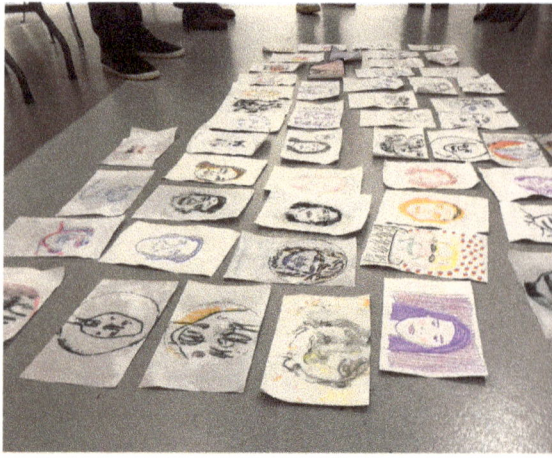

Example of a series of self portraits done in a workshop. Participants tried many different colors and designs.

Monoprints on Plexiglass

In art, a monotype or monoprint is a print taken from oil paint or ink and transferred onto glass or metal.

Making felt-tip-pen monotypes is an easy and fast way to make a drawing from a reference picture, and you can do it by using materials you most likely already have at home.

Once your artwork has dried, you may want to add more detail. Here are a few ideas to try:

For this exercise, you will need
- A sheet of glass or Plexiglass (the activity will work best if you lightly sand the surface of the Plexiglass to make it less slippery before beginning).
- Washable felt-tip pens
- Printing paper
- A spray bottle filled with water
- Tissue paper
- Fineliners, pastels, and other desired tools to add details to your drawing
- A printed reference picture (preferably at least 8 x 10 inches in size)

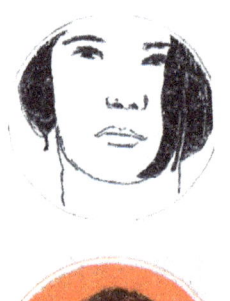
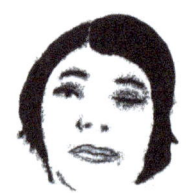
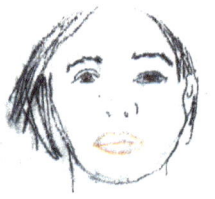
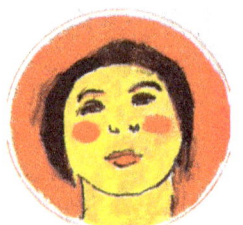
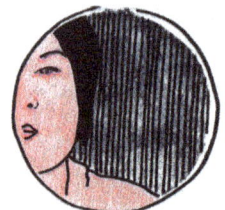
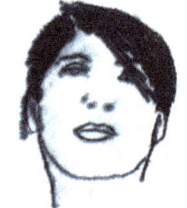

For this monoprint technique, we are using a felt-tip washable pen.

First, place your drawing underneath your glass or Plexiglass and then draw over your picture directly onto the surface. Here, you will choose what to keep in your print and what to leave out: because this technique is not as precise as a regular drawing, you may need to simplify your design.

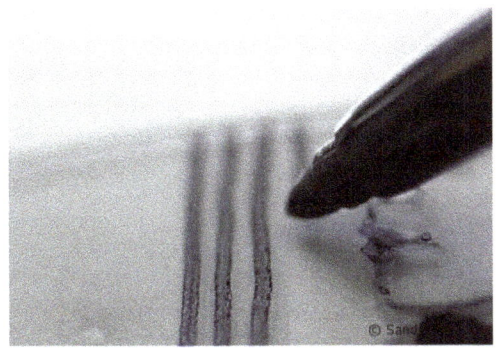

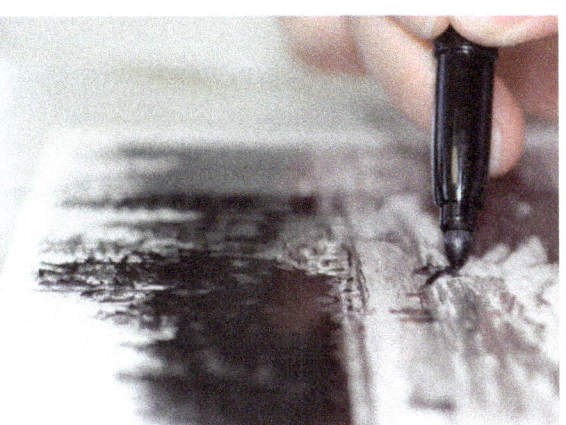

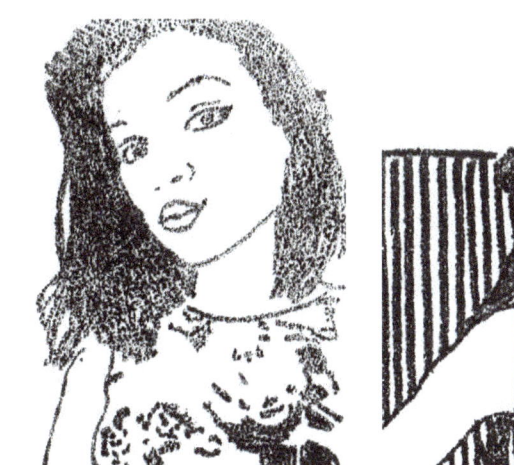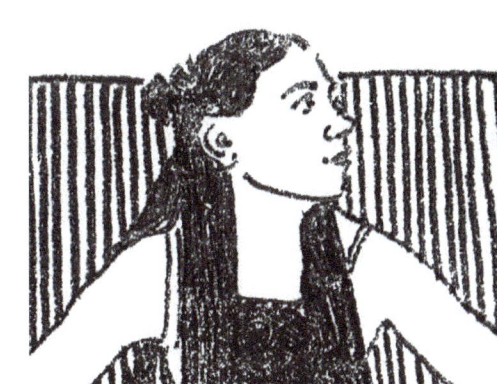

Example of monoprint portraits made on Plexiglass with felt pens.

The remainder of the exercise follows the steps of the "no-phone" selfie. Wet a piece of paper with a spray water bottle, dry it a bit with tissue paper, and apply it to the Plexiglass to make the monoprint.

 TIP:
You can use this same technique with watercolor pencils. The water in the wet paper will allow the watercolor pigment to transfer onto your work.

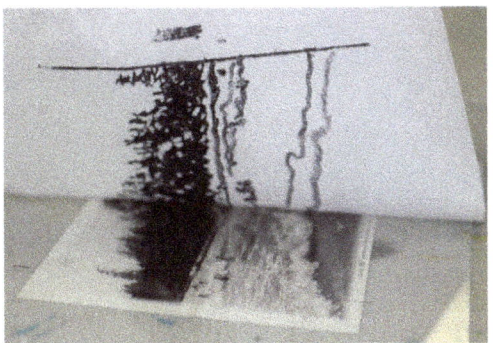

You can then add details or patterns that were not in your reference picture.

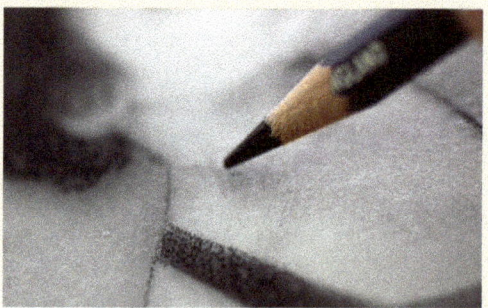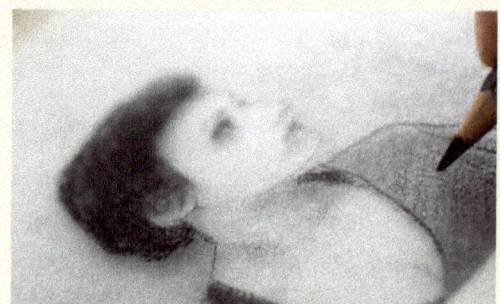

Example of drawing on Plexiglass with watercolor pencils

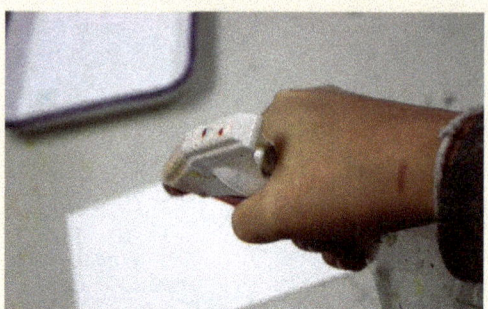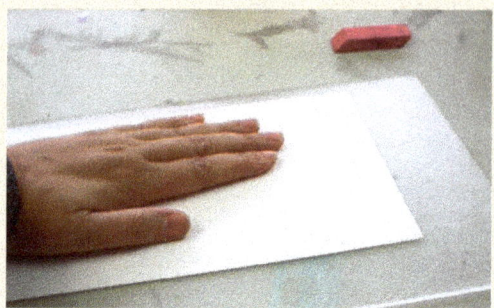

Example of making the monoprint by pressing the wet paper onto the surface

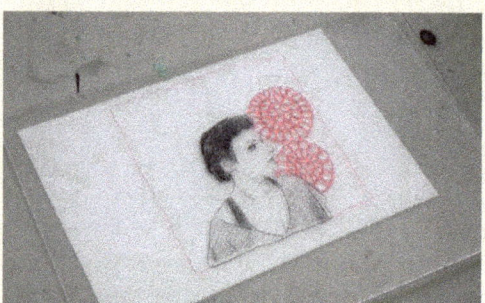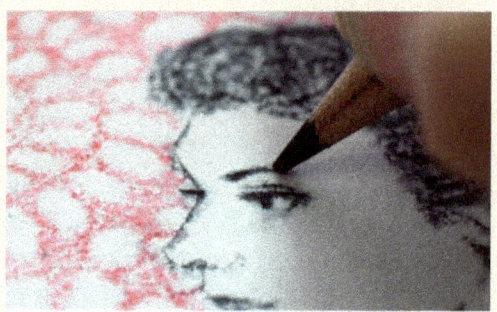

Adding details to the design.

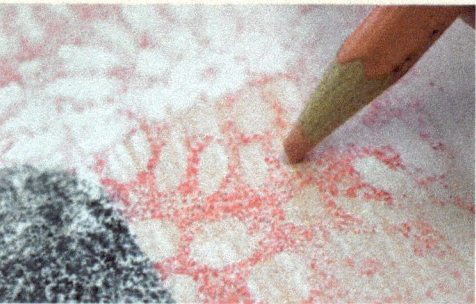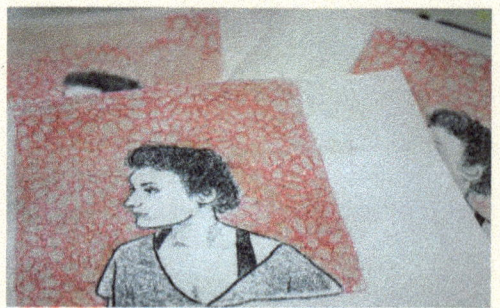

Adding color with colored pencils.

CHAPTER 14

Drawing From an Abstract Background

I like to paint from imagination, without any reference picture. It is a great way to feel free to express your inner world and imagery.

However, I still need a starting point to spark my imagination—and that support comes from an abstract background. Believe it or not, our brain dislikes nonsense and naturally tries to make sense of abstract shapes. All you have to do is relax, observe the background, and look for shapes that you can later outline and define.

For this exercise, you will need

- Paper (watercolor, bristol, or Yupo)
- Ink (I used India ink)
- A spray bottle filled with water
- A few brushes
- White acrylic paint
- Rubbing alcohol
- Markers, dry pastels, colored pencils, and other drawing tools you desire

Painting an Abstract Background

There are different ways you can experiment here: you can splash ink on wet paper, you can splash ink on dry paper and then spray it with water, or you can drip rubbing alcohol on top of a wet painted paper to add texture.

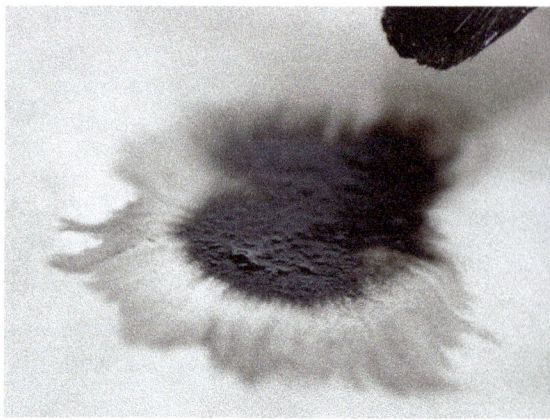

Example of dripping ink on wet paper.

Let your background dry. You might need to use a press or iron it on a low setting to make the paper flat again.

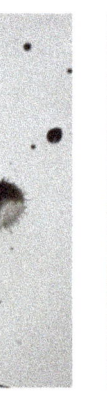
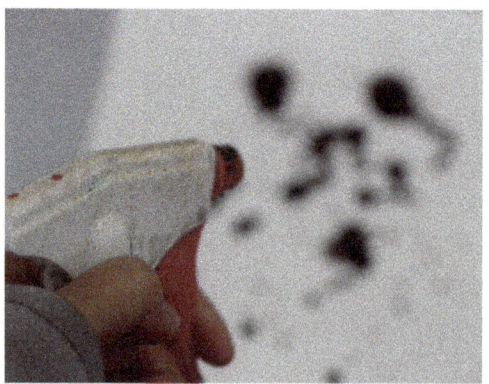
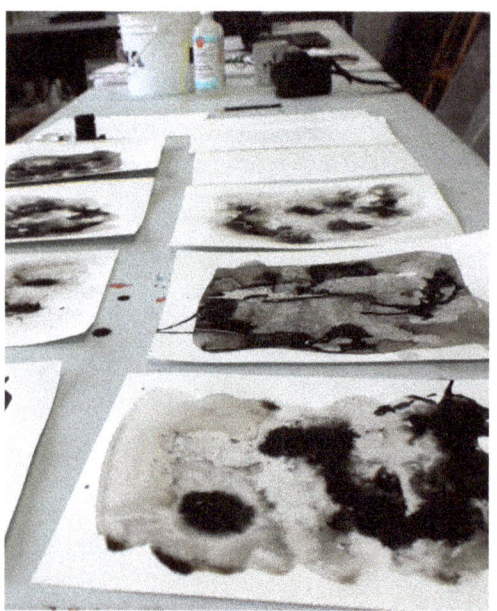

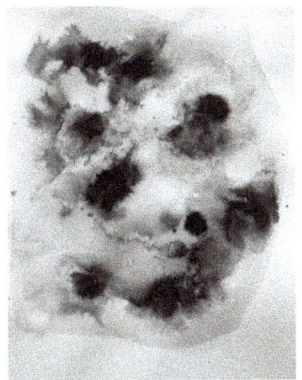 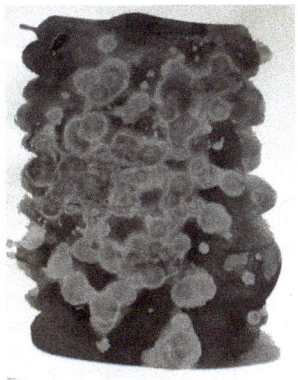 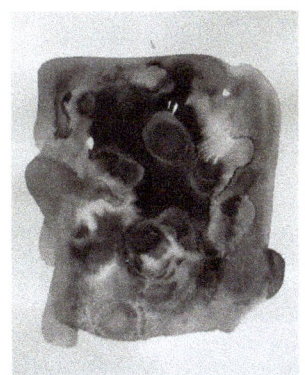 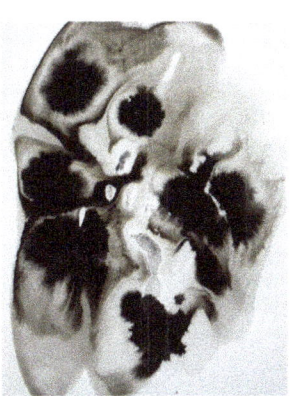

Examples of abstract backgrounds painted with India ink, water, and rubbing alcohol.

Identifying and Outlining Shapes

This is the fun part. Take a look at your background and try to find shapes within it. Most commonly, people will see faces, animals, underwater scenes, or flowers.

Once you start to see a shape emerge, outline it to separate it from the rest of the background. Don't worry if your shape is not perfect or is missing details—we will refine it in the next steps.

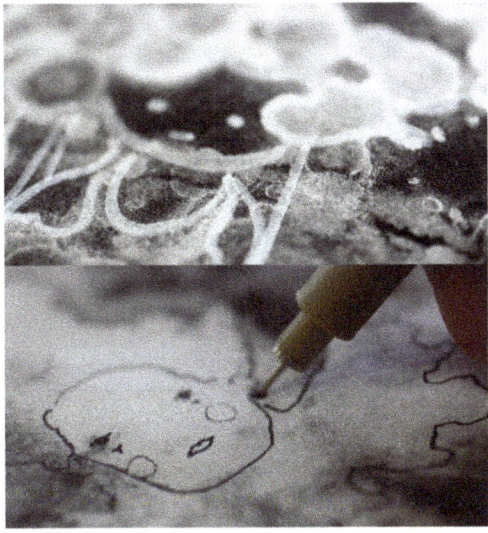

Example of outlining characters I see in the abstract background patterns.

Negative Painting with Acrylic

Next, you'll want to get rid of all the clutter and leave only the forms you've outlined. I like to use white acrylic here, but you can also use color.

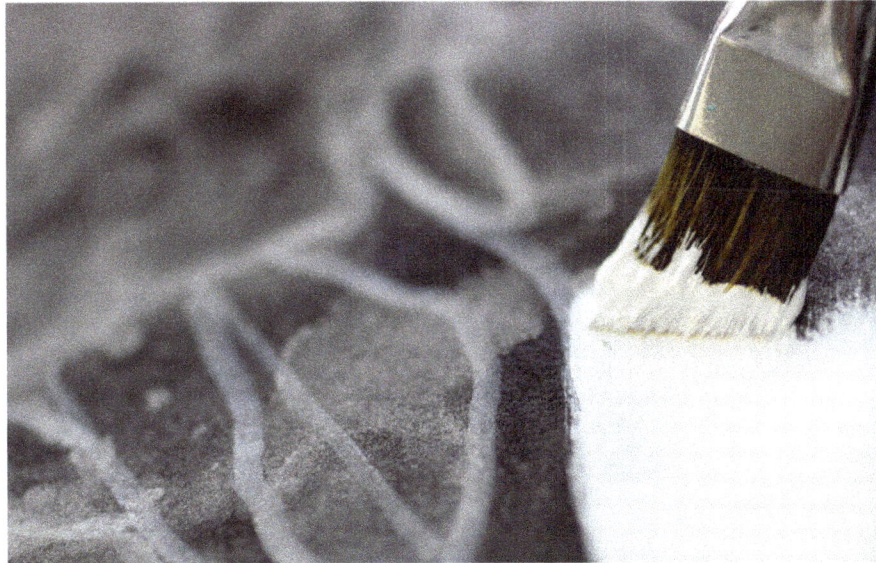

Example of painting around the shapes I outlined with white acrylic.

Refining and Adding Details

You can add darker color with a marker, like what I am doing here, to define hair or other dark elements.

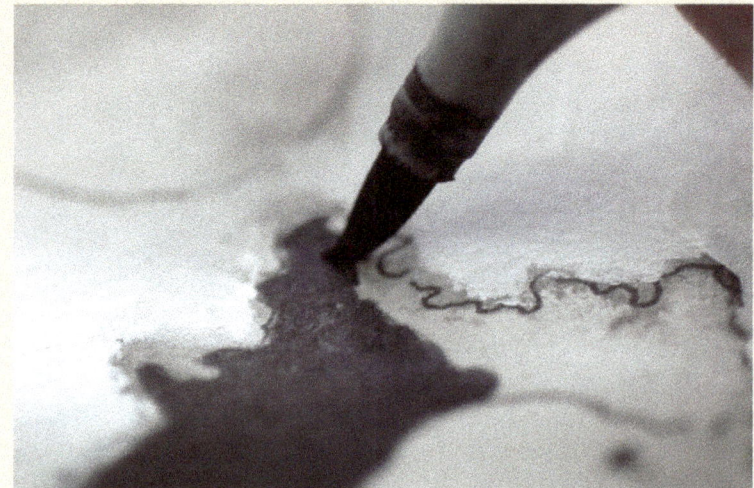

Here are some examples of characters I drew using this technique:

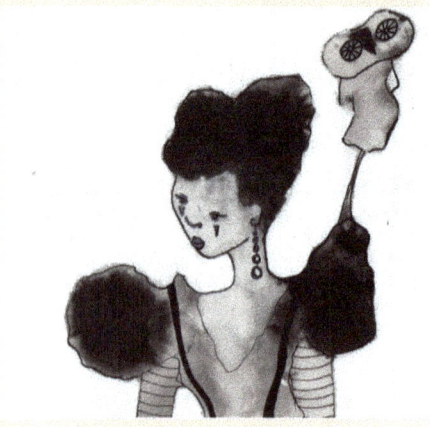

You can also add highlights with a dry pastel, for example.

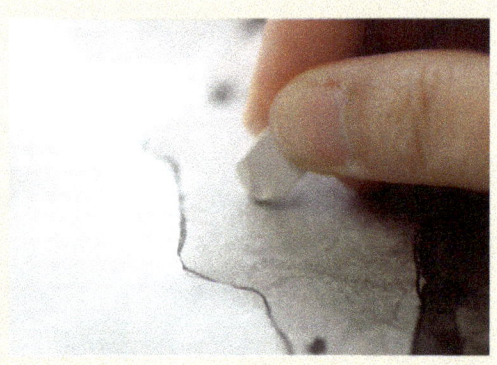

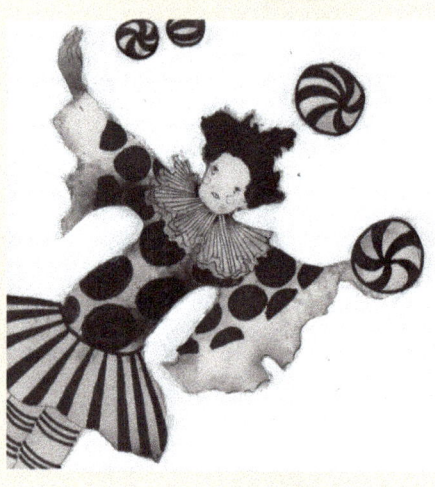

Try adding patterns in the background or on certain areas, like their clothing.

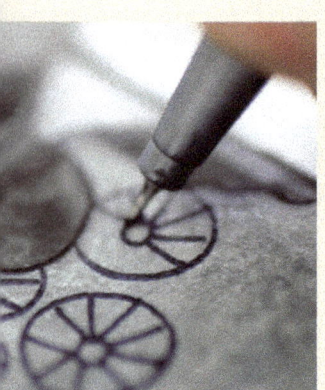
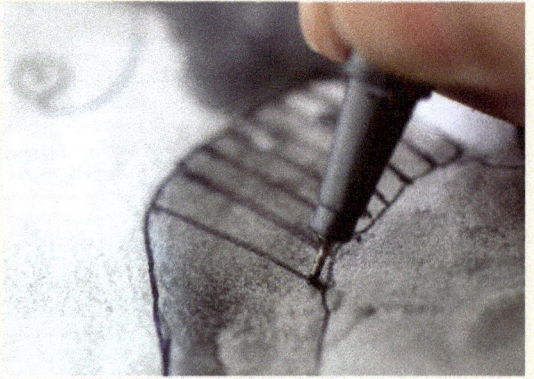

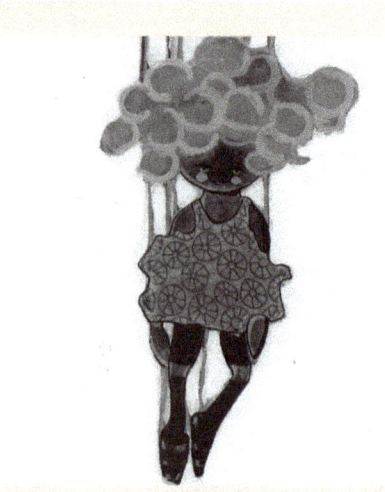

CHAPTER 15

Creative
Shading

Shading is what can make a drawing go from a flat contour drawing to a three-dimensional illusion.

There are many types of shading, and each will change the style of your drawing. Here are some of the basic types; try them on a simple sphere design as a fun exercise.

Cross-hatching

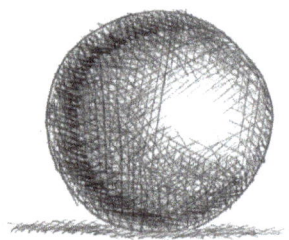

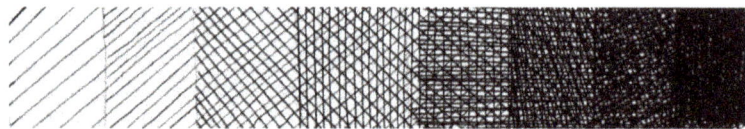

With cross hatching, you are drawing parallel lines that cross over one another and layering them to obtain varying intensities of shading. You can practice drawing a gradient of cross-hatching, like this:

I like to start with the lightest area and then add layers of cross-hatching until I reach the darkest area of the drawing.

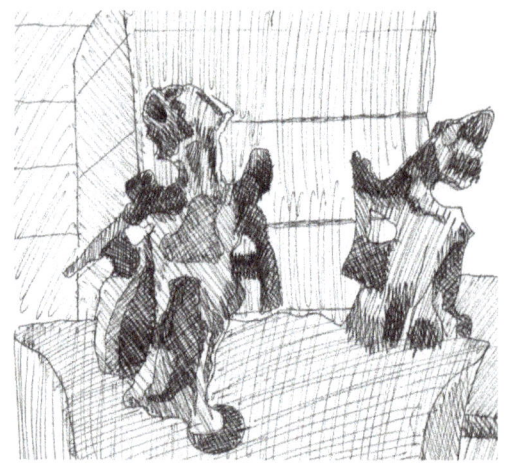

Example of a drawing of gargoyles on the roof of Notre-Dame de Paris using cross-hatching.

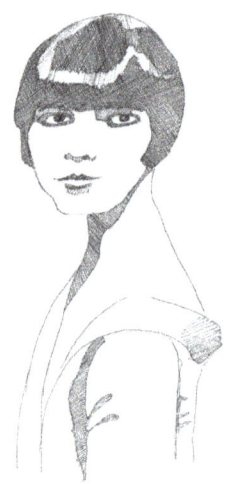

You can make your cross-hatching for portrait drawings as detailed as you want and achieve very high contrast.

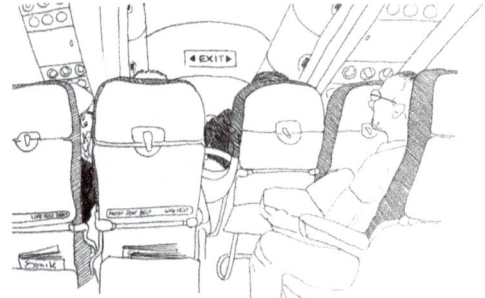

Cross-hatching also works well for quick sketches in ink.

Hatching with Parallel Lines

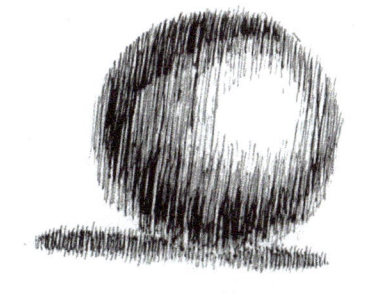

HATCHING.

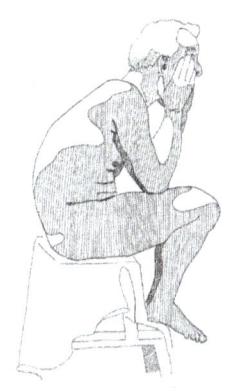
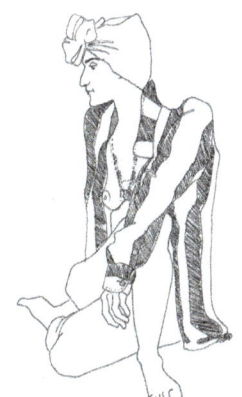

Example of parallel hatching in life drawings

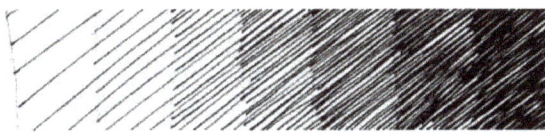

Hatching with parallel lines is the same as cross-hatching, except you are making all the lines in the same direction. It is a bit more time consuming than cross-hatching but can lead to interesting results.

Contour Lines

Contour lines can be created in many different ways. The idea is to draw lines that follow the shape of what you are drawing. You can use contour lines for shading, as in this example:

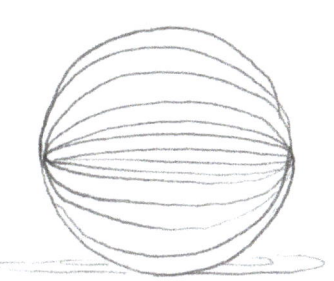

CONTOUR LINES

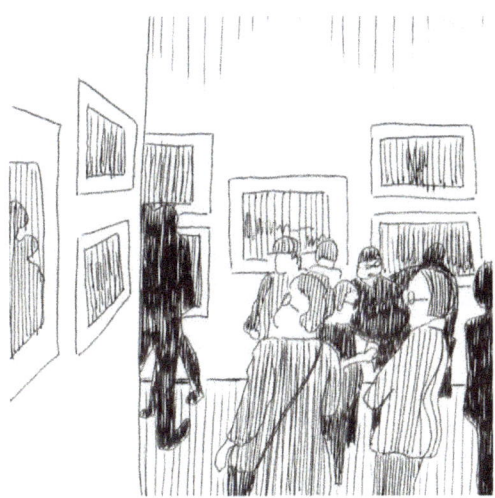

Example of hatching (shading with parallel lines)

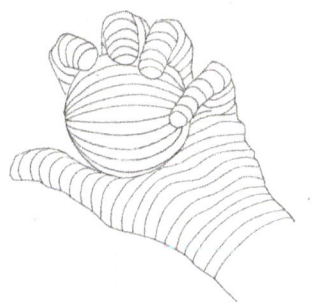
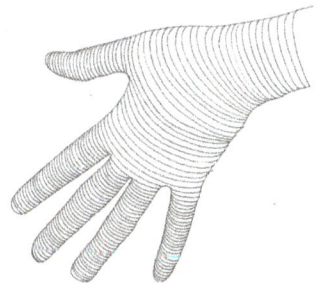

Contour lines work well on figure drawings.

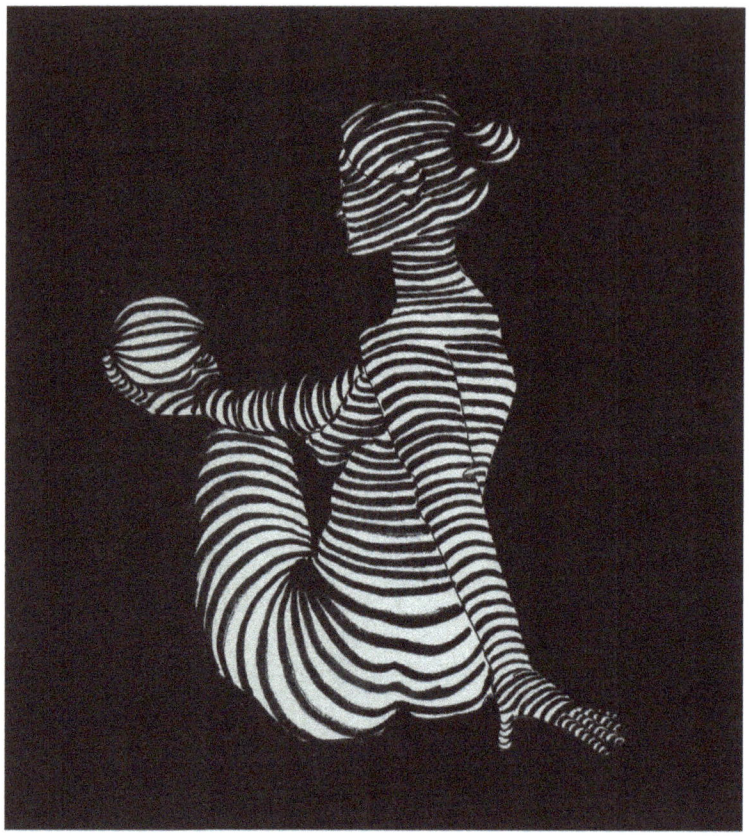

Example of contour lines on a figure drawing.

Scribbling

Scribbling (or scumbling) is a fun way to shade a drawing—and quick, too!

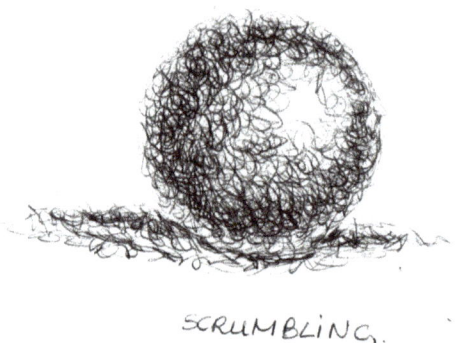

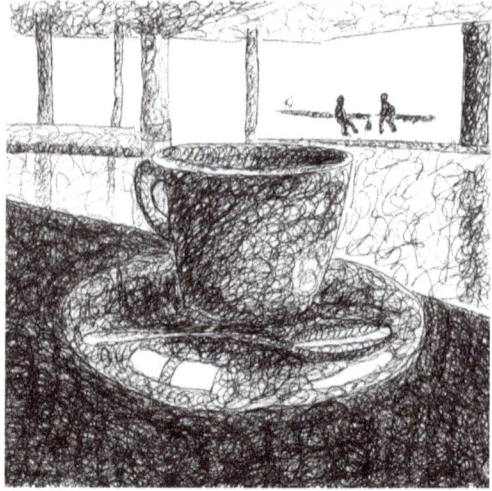

Scribble (or scumble) shading techniques work particularly well for portraits and still life.

For portraits, start by drawing an outline. Then, proceed to shade your drawing with a marker, using random movements of scribbling.

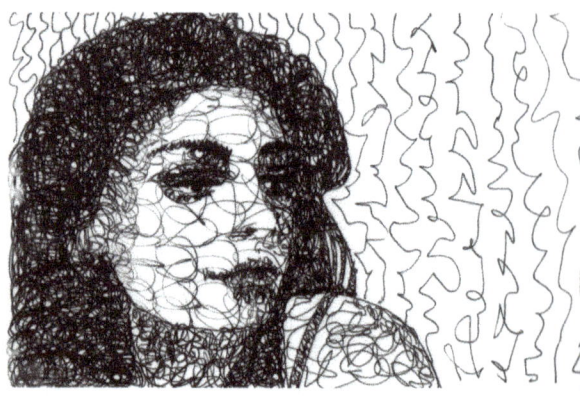

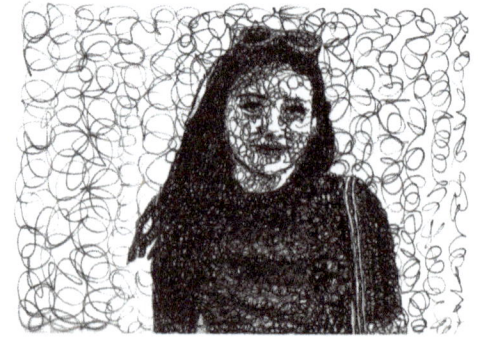

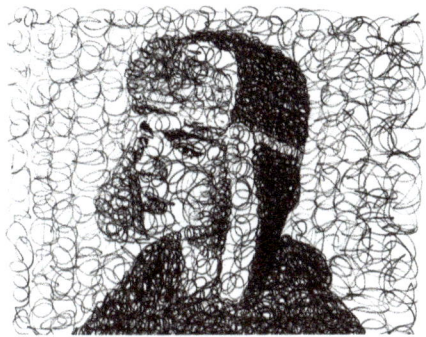

Stippling

Stippling is a fun technique, but it is very time consuming. I recommend you start by testing this technique on a smaller drawing first!

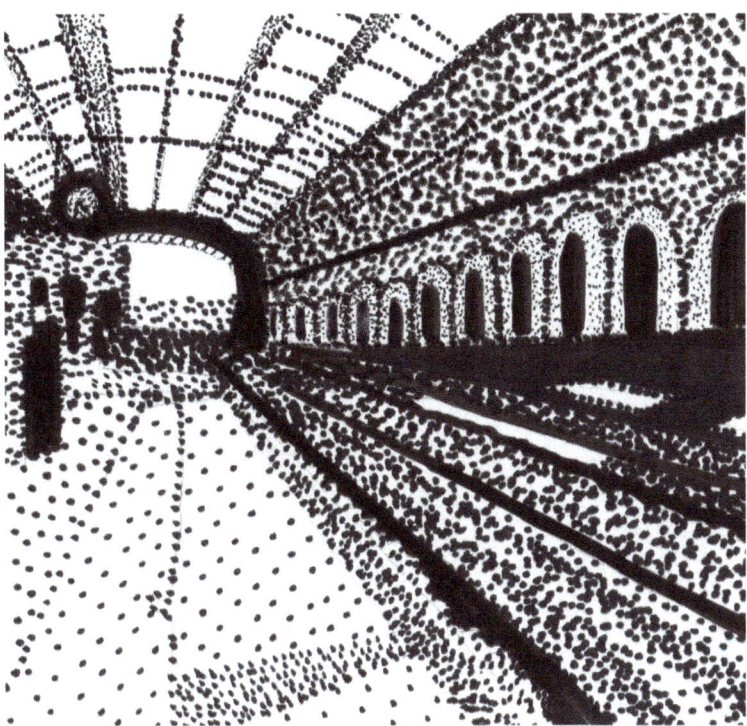

Example of a stippling drawing of a train station in France

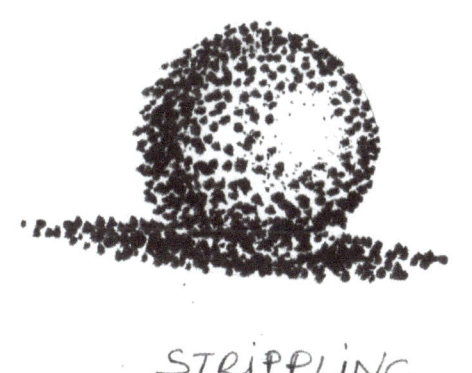

When using the stippling technique, use different marker sizes to make different sizes of dots throughout your piece.

Zentangles and Patterns

You can use any pattern you like for shading, including Zentangle-type patterns. Evaluate how dark your pattern will be, and fill the area corresponding to this shade with your Zentangle pattern.

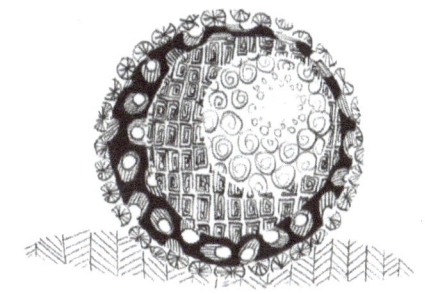

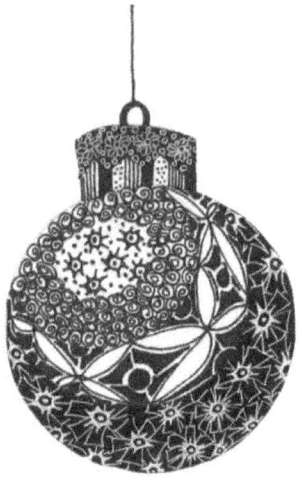

Drawing shaded with Zentangle patterns.

CHAPTER 16

Doodling Over Magazine Pages

It can be fun to transform ads filled with perfectly beautiful people and give them a more whimsical, out-of-the-box look! Even as a kid, I enjoyed making my own additions to the pictures on the TV guide.

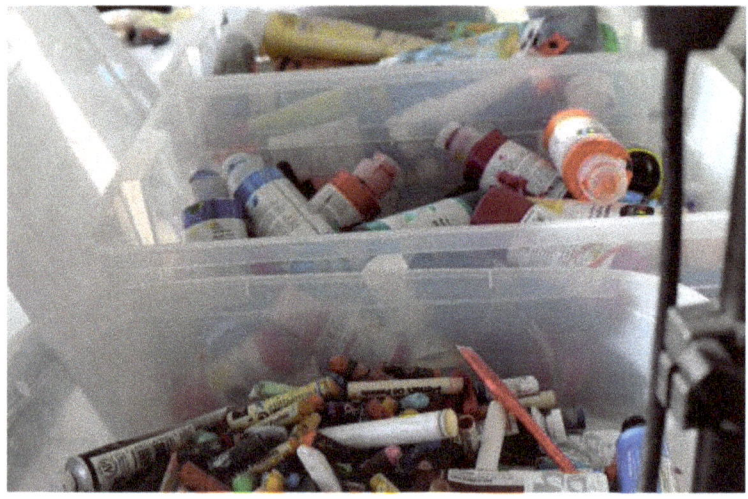

For this exercise, you can use just about any drawing tool:
- Acrylic paint
- Markers
- Oil pastels
- Fluid acrylics
- Colored pencils

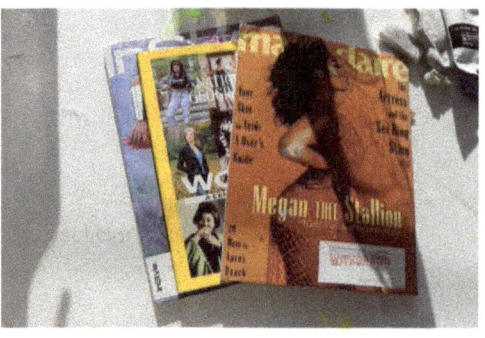

At many libraries, you can find magazines available at a very low price.

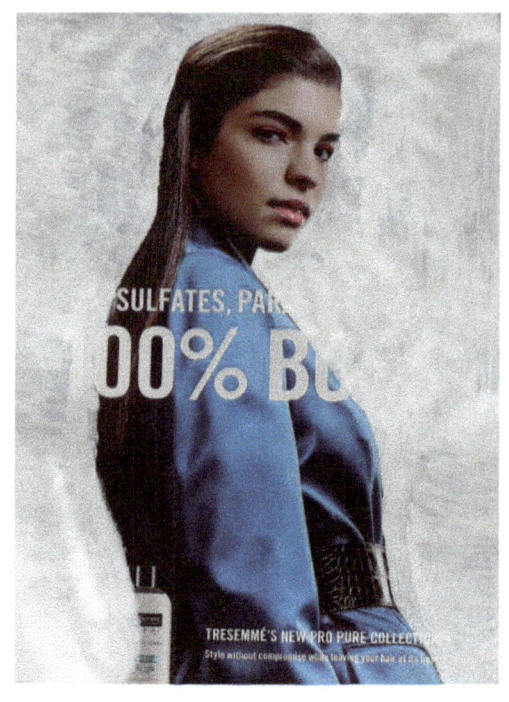

Begin by painting a layer of white acrylic paint over the background to remove distractions and highlight your figure.

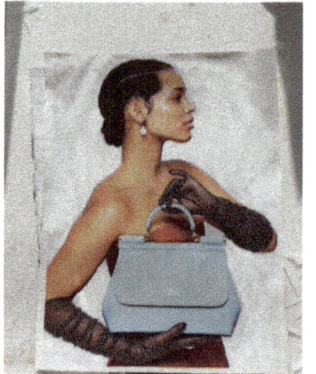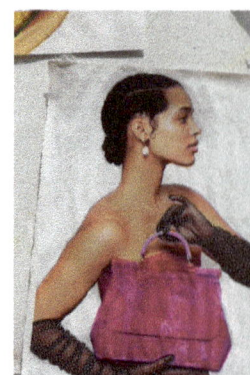

You can also block a figure's clothing and accessories with acrylic paint.

Next, add details; change the makeup, hair, and clothes.

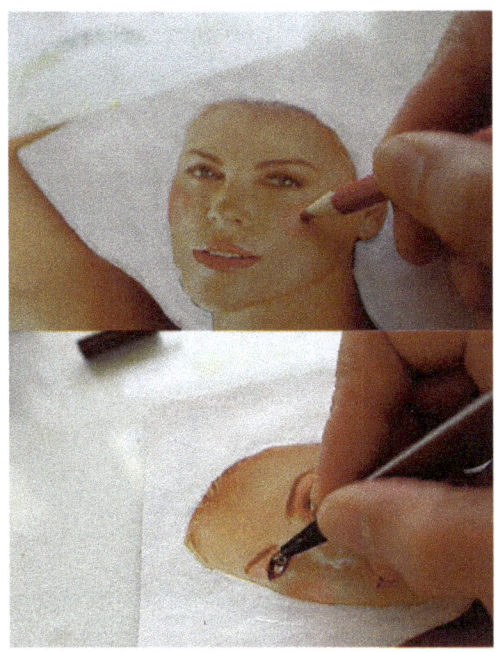

This is the fun part! I like to use fine-line markers for the makeup and markers or colored pencils for the round cheeks.

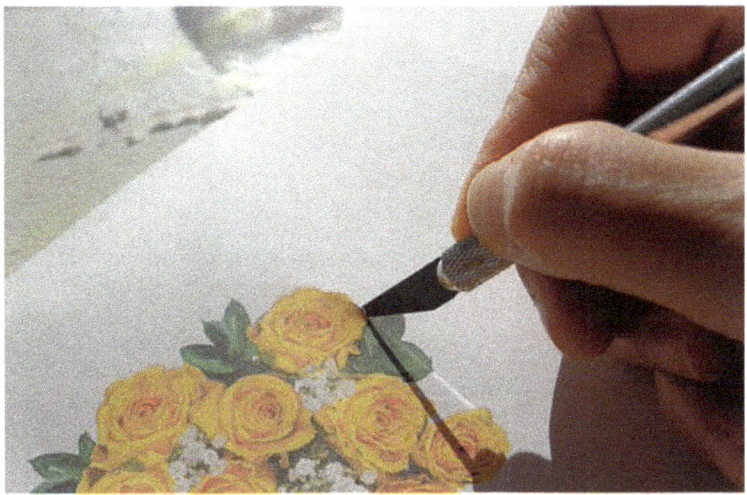

If your original magazine image is missing something ... collage it! Here, I wanted to add a pool cap with yellow roses on the model's head, so I printed a picture of yellow roses and collaged them onto the page.

Finally, work on the background.

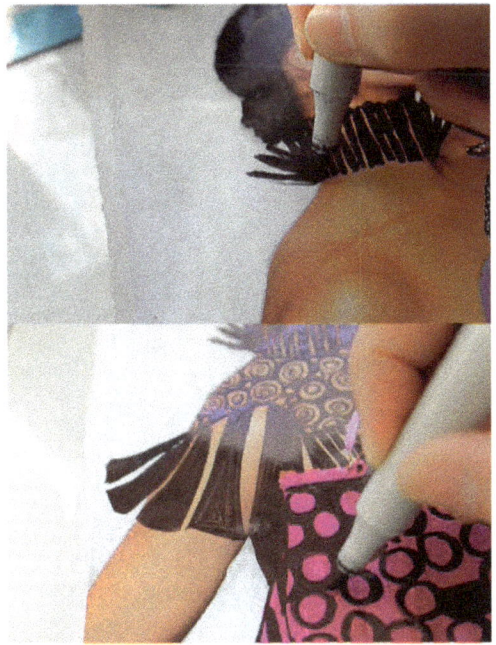

Here, I used a marker with a brush for the hair, clothes, and accessories.

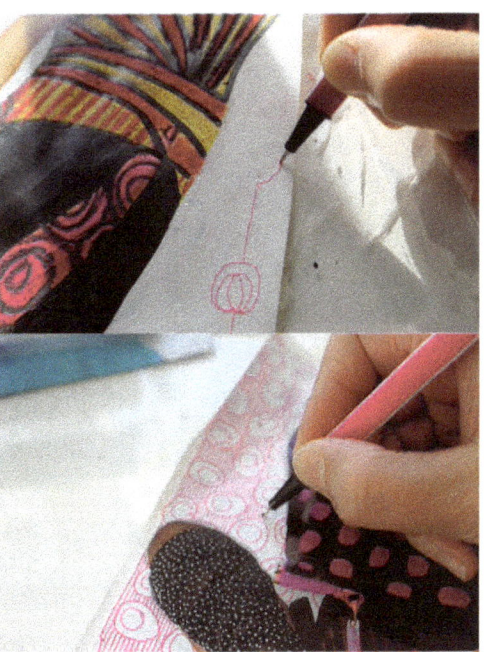

I love patterns, so here I added them with either a fine-line marker or oil pastels.

Most importantly, have fun! Here are a few examples of magazine covers I modified using this technique:

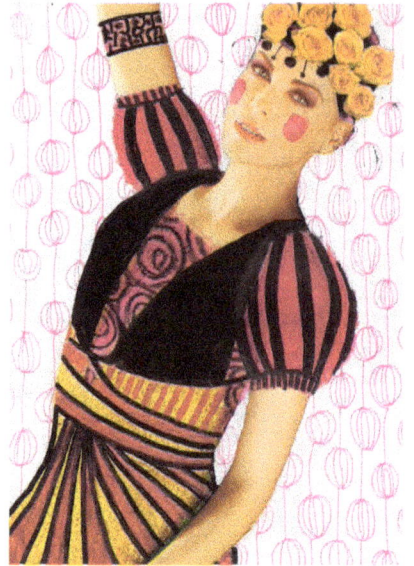
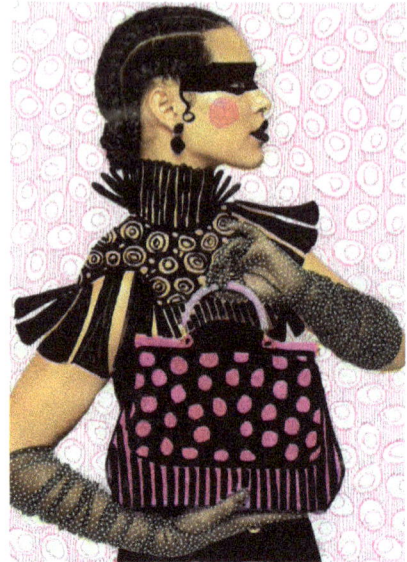
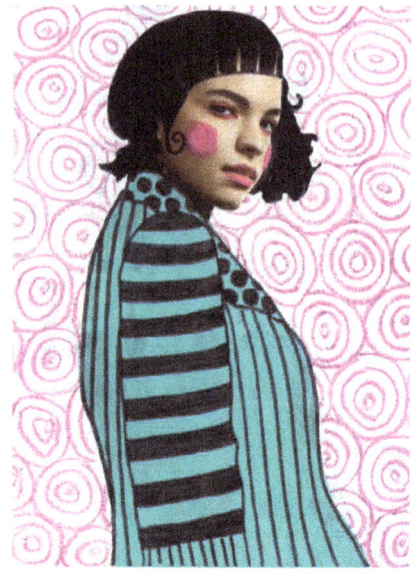

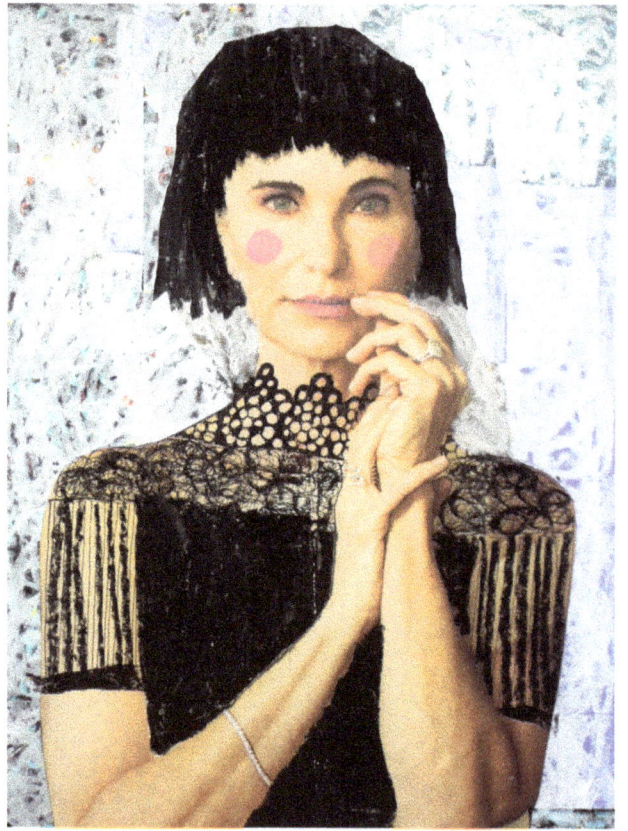
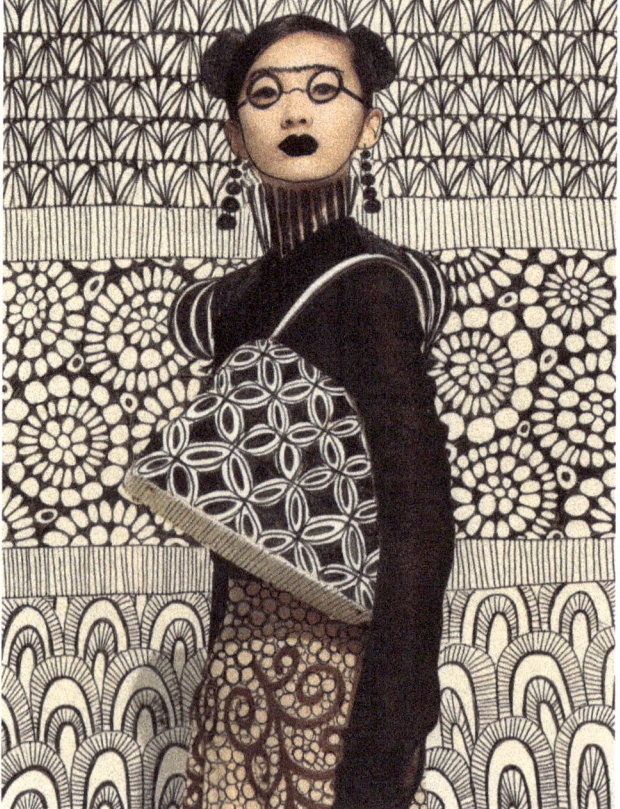

www.ingramcontent.com/pod-product-compliance
Lightning Source LLC
Chambersburg PA
CBHW061019280226
40342CB00004B/5